Why I Want to Leave

STRUGGLING WITH

EVANGELICALISM

and What It Takes to Stay

DAN STRINGER

Foreword by Richard J. Mouw

An imprint of InterVarsity Press
Downers Grove, Illinois

InterVarsity Press
P.O. Box 1400, Downers Grove, IL 60515-1426
ivpress.com
email@ivpress.com

InterVarsity Press® is the book-publishing division of InterVarsity Christian Fellowship/USA®, a movement of students and faculty active on campus at hundreds of universities, colleges, and schools of nursing in the United States of America, and a member movement of the International Fellowship of Evangelical Students. For information about local and regional activities, visit intervarsity.org.

All Scripture quotations, unless otherwise indicated, are taken from The Holy Bible, New International Version®, NIV®. Copyright © 1973, 1978, 1984, 2011 by Biblica, Inc.™ Used by permission of Zondervan. All rights reserved worldwide. www.zondervan.com. The "NIV" and "New International Version" are trademarks registered in the United States Patent and Trademark Office by Biblica, Inc.™

While any stories in this book are true, some names and identifying information may have been changed to protect the privacy of individuals.

The publisher cannot verify the accuracy or functionality of website URLs used in this book beyond the date of publication.

Cover design and image composite: Faceout Studio
Interior design: Jeanna Wiggins
Images: match © AlenKadr / Shutterstock Images
        nail © Lipskiy / Shutterstock Images

ISBN 978-0-8308-4766-2 (print)
ISBN 978-0-8308-4767-9 (digital)

Printed in the United States of America ∞

InterVarsity Press is committed to ecological stewardship and to the conservation of natural resources in all our operations. This book was printed using sustainably sourced paper.

Library of Congress Cataloging-in-Publication Data

Names: Stringer, Daniel, 1980- author.
Title: Struggling with evangelicalism : why I want to leave and what it
  takes to stay / Daniel Stringer.
Description: Downers Grove, IL : IVP, [2021] | Includes bibliographical
  references.
Identifiers: LCCN 2021030814 (print) | LCCN 2021030815 (ebook) I ISBN
  9780830847662 (paperback) | ISBN 9780830847679 (ebook)
Subjects: LCSH: Evangelicalism—United States. | Stringer, Daniel, 1980-
Classification: LCC BR1642.U5 S775 2021 (print) | LCC BR1642.U5 (ebook) |
  DDC 277.3/083—dc23
LC record available at https://lccn.loc.gov/2021030814
LC ebook record available at https://lccn.loc.gov/2021030815

P 25 24 23 22 21 20 19 18 17 16 15 14 13 12 11 10 9 8 7 6 5 4 3 2 1

Y 37 36 35 34 33 32 31 30 29 28 27 26 25 24 23 22 21

For my mother,

Linda Sook Yee Wong Stringer,

who introduced me to Jesus and
puts her faith into action
every day.

CONTENTS

FOREWORD

Richard Mouw

IT WAS GOOD FOR ME TO READ THIS BOOK. For one thing, Dan Stringer is an engaging writer. He has read widely; he thinks deeply—and he tells a good story.

But this book helped me understand some things that I have worried about in my own insistence that we not abandon the "evangelical" label. Evangelicalism has been good to me. It has paid my salary for the past half-century. More importantly it has given me a network of friends and organizations that I have been able to call "home" in my lifetime. I have had my quarrels, to be sure, but they have occurred for me within a spiritual and theological kinship system.

I realize, though, that a younger generation can easily interpret the defenses of the movement by folks like me as serving personal vested interests. Dan Stringer understands well the generational gap that is signaled in that dissent. He hears—and feels personally—the complaints of those who are distressed that "evangelical" has come to mean in many minds "right-wing extremism." He has personally felt the impatience with ongoing debates about whether there really is a viable "evangelical mind." And he is deeply offended by much-publicized reports of sexual scandals, gender abuse, and financial shenanigans. He has affinities with young professionals, campus ministry leaders, and women struggling with God's call in their lives, with whether to stick with it as evangelicals.

In the end, he personally decides in favor of "staying" in a movement that is, he says, "broken yet beautiful." He understands why others may choose differently, but for Dan, the remaining beauty makes it worth significant efforts to repair it: theologically, spiritually, and culturally. In accounting for what still attracts him to evangelicalism, he draws on his rich personal experience with global evangelicalism—the son of missionary parents, he lived in Asia and Africa for nine years of his youth.

Dan Stringer was once my student, but now he has become my teacher. I learned a lot from this book about both the brokenness and the beauty of the movement that I love. He also offers many wise, practical lessons about how to go about the necessary repair work. May it happen!

WHEN EVANGELICALISM IS YOUR MOTHER

WHEN I WAS A YOUNG CHILD, my parents read me a book called *Are You My Mother?* The story opens with a baby bird hatching from an egg while his mother is out finding food. Not knowing what his mother looks like, the hatchling waddles right past her. In successive encounters with a kitten, a dog, and a cow, the little bird asks, "Are you my mother?" To his dismay, they all reply no. Increasingly discouraged, the little bird begins to wonder if he even has a mother.

With escalating desperation, he calls out to a boat, an airplane, and an enormous power shovel, declaring, "Here I am, Mother," but not one answers. Finally, the power shovel drops him back into the nest, just as his mother returns and asks, "Do you know who I am?" The baby bird replies, "Yes, I know who you are. You are not a kitten. You are not a dog. You are not a cow. You are a bird, and you are my mother."

This heartwarming story centers on the search for a parent, but it's also a quest for identity. Until the baby bird knows who his mother is, he does not know who he is. Had he realized he was a bird, he would not have asked the other animals if they were his mother. Without an accurate self-understanding, he looks for belonging among boats, airplanes, and power shovels. The hatchling is not just looking for his mother; he is looking for his identity.

Like baby birds waddling from the nest, evangelical Christians sometimes don't know which species of *Christian* they are. They might identify broadly as Christians but don't see themselves belonging to the *evangelical* category. Lacking awareness of who laid the egg from which they hatched, they don't realize that evangelicalism is their mother. Like the bird who hatched while his mama was away, they walk right past their evangelical parents and siblings without recognizing them as family. When they hear the word *evangelical* used to describe something narrow-minded and negative, they think to themselves, "That's not me!"

Part of what makes *Are You My Mother?* a compelling children's story is the comparisons between incongruent things. Dogs and cats are not birds. Boats and planes are not animals. As young children learn to distinguish between different kinds of objects, they are technically learning what is called *taxonomic differentiation*. Tables and chairs are both furniture but different kinds. Bananas and mangoes are both fruits, but taxonomic differentiation helps kids understand that mangoes aren't the only kind of fruit.

Evangelicalism could use more taxonomic differentiation these days. It is not the only place on Christianity's big map, yet those of us who consider ourselves evangelical may not realize that our way of following Jesus is just one form of Christianity rather than the whole thing. While it's common for evangelicals in the United

States to identify themselves simply as "Christians," this has downsides. First, it confuses a larger category (Christian) with a smaller category (evangelical Protestant). Catholics, Protestants, and Eastern Orthodox believers are all Christians but practice their faith differently. The majority of Christians in the world are not Protestants, much less evangelical Protestants (see figure 0.1).[1] Furthermore, three in five evangelicals live in Asia or Africa, whereas less than one in five live in North American (see figure 0.2).[2]

Second, it fails to acknowledge evangelicalism's particularity as a space within Christianity. Evangelical norms like informal, extemporaneous prayer ("Good morning, Lord") are taken for granted as the Christian standard and thus are simply deemed "prayer" without an adjective, whereas non-evangelical styles of prayer are referred to with greater precision, like contemplative prayer or liturgical prayer. Third, it claims supremacy for itself at the expense of other expressions of Christianity, as if evangelicals have a monopoly on Jesus. If we take seriously the body of Christ's diversity worldwide, neither *Christian* nor *Protestant* are specific enough terms to identify our particular faith tradition.

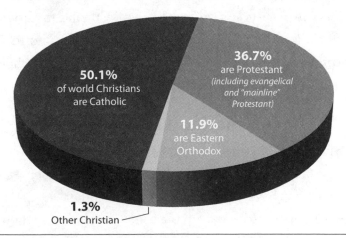

Figure 0.1

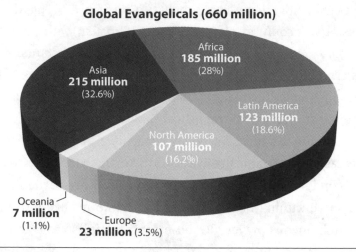

Global Evangelicals (660 million)

Asia 215 million (32.6%)

Africa 185 million (28%)

Latin America 123 million (18.6%)

North America 107 million (16.2%)

Oceania 7 million (1.1%)

Europe 23 million (3.5%)

Figure 0.2

For evangelicals who see themselves as Christianity's default setting, developing a healthy self-awareness requires situating evangelicalism as a particular location on a bigger map. When we fail to acknowledge our own particularity, we're like baby birds who haven't looked in the mirror to see that we have feathers, wings, and beaks. We run the risk of assuming that all animals live in nests and lay eggs like we do. Unable to recognize our flock, we wander in search of belonging, hoping to find someone who will claim us as their own. Until we learn who our mother is, we can't know who we are.

MOTHER CHURCH

St. Cyprian of Carthage, a North African bishop from the third century, famously said, "No one can have God for their Father, who does not have the Church for their mother." At the time, many were splitting away from the church because they thought it had compromised its identity by readmitting those who previously bowed to false gods. Cyprian strongly opposed such a split, contending there could only be one true and united church. Imagine what Cyprian would say about the plethora of denominations in today's evangelical landscape! Instead of seeing God our Father wedded to the church our mother, evangelicals have so emphasized a personal and direct relationship with God that we've stopped recognizing the church as our mother. When we treat the church as a consumer product whose purpose is to satisfy religious customers, we've lost sight of the church as our mother.

My earliest church memories recall the sound of acoustic guitars strumming chords to *Maranatha!* worship choruses like "Jesus, Name Above All Names" and "Seek Ye First" sung in our living room—a house church my parents helped start in the early 1980s. At the age of six, I prayed to ask Jesus into my heart. Like most six-year-old evangelical kids, I couldn't have understood that my church home was merely one of many congregations belonging to one of many denominations, each representing different ways of doing church. I didn't yet know that Christianity wasn't started by English-speaking Americans. All I knew was that I wanted Jesus in my heart—a very evangelical thing to desire!

When I was seven, my parents put their evangelical faith into action by signing on as Presbyterian medical missionaries sent from the United States to Zaïre, now known as the Democratic Republic of the Congo (DRC).[3] We moved from Mililani, Hawai'i, to Jonquiere, Quebec, for an immersion year of learning French. We spent the next three years living in Kananga, Zaïre, followed by eighteen months back in Hawai'i, then a six-month stint in Kentucky before living in Kathmandu, Nepal, for six years. During the last three of those years, I attended Faith Academy, an inter-denominational, evangelical boarding school in Manila, Philip-pines. By the time I graduated from high school, I had lived in five countries on three continents—largely due to my family's evangelical faith.

If growing up in Africa and Asia as an American missionary kid isn't a full-scale evangelical upbringing, I don't know what is. My parents put their personal faith into public action. As each move made it harder to identify home, our family's faith became the common thread between otherwise incongruent chapters in a nomadic upbringing. As a teenager, I coped with the disconnect from US culture by latching on to any artifact of American Chris-tianity I could get my hands on. Having treasured *McGee and Me!* videos and *Adventures in Odyssey* cassette tapes during my ele-mentary years, I naturally progressed to evangelical teen maga-zines like *Breakaway* and *Campus Life*, while stockpiling albums by my favorite Christian rock bands like DC Talk and Audio Adrenaline. If I couldn't live in the United States like most American-born teenagers, I could at least prepare myself to re-enter US culture after high school.

One question drove my college search process: Which school would give me the best chance of finding other mis-sionary kids who took their faith as seriously as I did? A rush of excitement and joy flooded me as I opened my acceptance letter from Wheaton College. I didn't realize it at the time, but I had embarked on a quest to put down roots inside evangeli-calism, the only consistent home I knew. Like the hatchling in *Are You My Mother?,* I needed to know where I came from. Not only was I searching for evangelicalism, I was searching for myself.

A TROUBLED BRAND

It wasn't until college that the word *evangelical* entered my vocabulary. My first semester at Wheaton, I took a class called "Theology of Culture" taught by the late Tim Phillips. I remember Dr. Phillips passing out index cards on which he instructed freshman students to identify their denominational background. I found this exercise almost as challenging as explaining (in under ten minutes) where I grew up. Until age seven, my family belonged to a house church planted through the United Church of Christ, a denomination whose history in Hawai'i dates back to congregationalist missionaries arriving from New England in 1820. While living abroad, my parents worked for a Presbyterian denomination, but we didn't regularly attend a Presbyterian church. Most of these years, we attended international Protestant churches comprised of Western missionaries from a wide range of church backgrounds.

Unsure of my denominational identity but trying to fit in with my new classmates, I wrote "nondenominational" on the index card. This choice felt safe enough, but notice the irony. Despite being raised by devout evangelical parents who literally crossed the globe for their faith, I didn't know I was an evangelical before taking Dr. Phillips's class at age eighteen! In fact, I don't recall anyone during my childhood informing me that the type of Christianity we practiced had a name: *evangelicalism*.

When Lifeway Research surveyed the differences between those who call themselves evangelicals and those who hold evangelical beliefs, they found a gap. While the two groups overlap, there are notable differences. More Americans self-identify as evangelicals (24%) than strongly agree with evangelical beliefs (15%). At the same time, a significant number of evangelical believers reject the term "evangelical." Around two-thirds (69%) of evangelicals by belief self-identify as evangelicals, whereas one-third do not.[4]

The study also found that race and ethnicity play a role in the labels Christians use. African Americans make up 23 percent of those who hold evangelical beliefs but only 14 percent of those who self-identify as evangelical. They are also more likely to identify as "born again" (49 percent) than whites (27 percent), Hispanics (24 percent), or those of other ethnicities (19 percent). This is despite the fact that African Americans (30 percent) are more than twice as likely to hold evangelical beliefs than whites (13 percent), Hispanics (13 percent), or those of other ethnicities (9 percent).

If 31 percent of American evangelical believers reject the label, it's no surprise that other terms are used when self-identifying one's faith. In fact, it's perfectly possible to love Jesus, read the Bible, and belong to a church with evangelical beliefs without ever having to think of oneself as an evangelical or self-identify with more precision than "Christian." This doesn't feel too imprecise within evangelicalism but probably wouldn't be the case outside of it. Can you imagine a Catholic not knowing they are Catholic? It would be almost unimaginable for Catholics, Mormons, or Muslims in the United States not to identify with their religious faith group. The more you understand about global Christianity's diversity, the more you see that neither *Christian* nor *Protestant* are sufficiently specific terms when identifying evangelicalism.

Why don't more Christians with evangelical beliefs self-identify as evangelicals? We've already looked at one factor, the custom of elevating ourselves to Christianity's default setting (especially in places where we're prevalent enough to get away with it). Another barrier is our aversion to the word's negative connotations, summarized by Mark Labberton:

The word "evangelical" has morphed from being commonly used to describe a set of theological and spiritual commitments into a passionately defended, theo-political brand. Worse, that brand has become synonymous with social arrogance, ignorance and prejudice—all antithetical to the gospel of Jesus Christ.[5]

In the fall of 2008, I began my first semester of grad school, pursuing a master's degree in social work at the University of Hawai'i. Political conversations weren't uncommon on campus, especially leading up to that year's presidential election. One evening after class, I found myself in such an exchange while walking to the parking lot alongside several classmates. As we discussed a recent debate between candidates Barack Obama and John McCain, we all agreed that then-Senator Obama had articulated many of the concerns relevant to social workers, including poverty, healthcare access, and education. The conversation rolled smoothly until one of my classmates remarked, "Things would be so much better if wasn't for all those [expletive] evangelicals."

I understood what he meant but didn't appreciate his sweeping characterization. After all, my faith in Jesus factored prominently in my social work interests. Unsure of what to say, I tried to explain that all evangelicals don't necessarily vote alike. Was it worth outing myself as an evangelical in the hope of nuancing his opinion? I don't remember my words, but I vividly recall feeling awkward and anxious as I tried to reconcile my positive experiences inside evangelicalism with its negative political reputation.

If identifying as evangelical was difficult in 2008, the years since have only made the label easier to disavow. The morning

after 81 percent of white evangelical voters helped elect Donald
Trump to the American presidency in 2016, a Fuller Seminary
professor posted on social media, "I won't be calling myself an
evangelical anymore in the future, or struggling to reinterpret
the term in a better way."[6] Five days later, Katelyn Beaty, former
managing editor of *Christianity Today* wrote, "When it comes to
the Bible and Jesus and evangelism and service, the 81 percent
and I share the same DNA.... But this time, this election, I can't
defend my people. I barely recognize them."[7]

For Rev. Sandra Maria Van Opstal, a second-generation Latina
born to immigrants from Colombia and Argentina, the experience was less about her response to evangelicals and more
about evangelicals' response to her. Pastor Van Opstal identifies
evangelicalism as "the spiritual heritage of my rebirth and the
tradition where my immediate family members find themselves
even today. It's not that I can't include myself with evangelicals.
Rather, evangelicals have not sought to include me."[8] She recalls
an example of her frustration with a predominately white evangelical institution: "Despite the tens of thousands of pages I read
while in seminary, I was never assigned a book by an ethnic minority scholar, let alone a Latinx theologian."[9]

Much ink was spilled on white evangelicalism's role in the
2016 election, yet why was so little attention given to how evangelicals of color voted? Despite the fact that one-third of
American evangelicals aren't white, prevailing connotations of
evangelical fail to account for this diversity.[10] As an Asian
American, it took considerable effort to find statistics on how my
subgroup voted. When the only evangelicals being counted are
white, it's no surprise this term has come to signify an increasingly narrow slice of Christianity. A whitewashed evangelical

brand not only fails to reflect evangelicals of color, it's also more susceptible to being co-opted by a racist, sexist, anti-immigrant agenda that looks almost nothing like Jesus.

For those hoping to liberate evangelicalism from its brand name of ill repute, the solution appears simple: drop the label. If it harms our credibility, hinders our witness, and creates barriers to being accurately understood, why keep it in our vocabulary? If the term represents nothing more than the latest iteration of white nationalist idolatry and injustice, shouldn't Jesus' followers keep their distance? If this word repels and confuses the neighbors God instructs us to love, why not abandon it? Furthermore, why should Christians of color use a term that has historically placed white Christians at the center?

I'm sympathetic to concerns about our credibility and public witness. If evangelicalism was only a brand, I'd support exchanging it for something better. There's only one problem: Evangelicalism isn't just a brand. It is also a space.

A SHARED SPACE

One can drop the evangelical label while continuing to reside in evangelical spaces. Evangelical identity is more than a T-shirt hanging on the religious clothing rack, something to put on or take off depending on your desired look. Evangelicalism is more than a billboard or logo. The adjective *evangelical* is indispensable because it points to a vital entity—the noun *evangelicalism*— a space within Christianity that includes more than 60 million believers in the United States[11] and half a billion worldwide.[12] Not only is evangelicalism the mother of many children, she's also the place where most of them live. The evangelical brand may have lost its appeal, but evangelical spaces aren't going away anytime soon.

Brands and spaces overlap, but they don't align perfectly. Take the United States, for instance. The country's "brand" includes Uncle Sam, Lady Liberty, a bald eagle, and imagery of stars and stripes. This brand distinguishes the United States from other countries, but its symbols don't resonate with all inhabitants. Some Americans are put off by this brand because it doesn't reflect their experience and concerns. The message communicated by America's brand may not represent everyone from the United States. Similarly, not everyone inside evangelicalism identifies with its brand. It's perfectly possible, if not increasingly common, to reject the label without leaving the space. You can be part of evangelicalism's *demographics* (quantifiable traits of a population that can be observed from the outside) without necessarily conforming to its *psychographics* (internal motives and values that drive behavior).

In late 2017, an African American professor of missiology from an evangelical university in Illinois visited an evangelical seminary in California to preach for their weekly chapel service. During his sermon, the professor emphatically declared, "I am no longer an evangelical. I handed my divorce papers to evangelicalism last November because . . . I've spent the better half of my career pleading and begging with white evangelicals [for space] . . . I'm done begging. . . . I'm tired of asking white folks for permission to say something."[13]

What should we make of an accomplished Christian scholar, educated and employed by evangelical institutions, declaring to an evangelical audience that he is now done with evangelicalism? I take him to mean that he's done with the brand but not the space. And who can blame him? Like this professor, I, too, am repulsed by the whitewashed evangelical brand in its most recent iteration, yet I continue making my spiritual home in the place known as American evangelicalism. It's not my brand of choice, but it's the space where I live.

Instead of a brand, consider what happens when we think of evangelicalism primarily as a shared space.

- A brand is disposable depending on personal preferences, but a shared space requires collective responsibility for its care over the long haul.

- A brand depends on satisfying individual consumers— especially those with buying power, but a shared space is accessible to a broad range of inhabitants.

- A brand promotes itself through slogans and celebrity endorsements, but a shared space offers opportunities to build relationships across differences and divisions.

- A brand is no use to those who don't like it, but a shared space can be home for a diverse range of people, including those who don't fit the brand.

OWNING OUR BAGGAGE

Once we re-envision evangelicalism as a common space, we start noticing how its well-being impacts residents. When a neighborhood's crime rate spikes or water supply becomes contaminated, concerned residents take collective responsibility for addressing the problem. Instead of calling it someone else's responsibility or waiting for it to get worse, they take action on behalf of their community. Like any place, evangelicalism has its fair share of problems and unhealthy patterns that disproportionately harm residents on the margins. I call this our "baggage." Every religious group has baggage, but things get worse when we fail to own it as ours. When problems are identified inside evangelicalism (especially in the United States), we're quick to say, "Glad that's not my neighborhood." It's much easier to shout advice from a safe distance than participate in a messy cleanup.

Our aversion to the evangelical label makes it harder to own our baggage. I sometimes joke that you can tell someone is an evangelical if they strive to not be known as an evangelical. To keep our baggage at a distance, we attach prefixes and qualifiers like neo-evangelical, post-evangelical, progressive evangelical, big tent evangelical, postmodern evangelical, and even sorta-evangelical. In the United States, our prevalence grants us the privilege to self-define in ways that keep the mess at arm's length. Just as racial and gender privilege have facilitated the hijacking of evangelicalism's brand, it also takes a certain degree of *religious* privilege to have the option of rebranding when we don't like how it looks on us. "Those aren't my people," we say, but not every religious group has that option. Here's a thought experiment: When Catholics, Mormons, or Muslims are negatively stereotyped, misunderstood, or face fallout from a scandal, can they swap out their name to increase favorability ratings? Not in the United States, they can't.

When we know where our neighborhood ends and another begins, it becomes easier to take care of the place we call home. Despite my uneasiness with much of what American evangelicalism is known for, I have a responsibility that comes with living here. I was born here, work here, and raise my kids here. Many loved ones live here too. It's our spiritual home, the place where we met Jesus and became his disciples. Evangelicalism's problems might look obvious from the outside, but they aren't being well addressed from the inside. I'm often embarrassed by what happens in my religious neighborhood, which is why I'm trying to leave this place better than I found it. Make no mistake: there's a big mess to clean up in American evangelicalism, but it starts with admitting we live here.

1

STRUGGLING WITH EVANGELICALISM

EVANGELICALISM IS MY SPIRITUAL HABITAT. I graduated from Wheaton College and Fuller Seminary. I work for Inter-Varsity Christian Fellowship. My local congregation belongs to the Evangelical Covenant Church, the denomination that ordained me to pastoral ministry. I read publications like *Christianity Today*, support the work of agencies like World Vision, and can rattle off the lyrics to just about any worship song in the CCLI Top 100. For better or worse, my spiritual zipcode lies deep inside evangelicalism. In many ways, I benefit from the evangelical status quo. And I am conflicted about that.

Maybe you're struggling with evangelicalism too. If so, it could be for any number of reasons. Perhaps you're disillusioned with the political platform that's been conflated with Christianity into a package deal. Or you're grappling with how a seemingly

Christ-centered apologist like Ravi Zacharias could have sexually abused so many victims by using his ministry as leverage. Even if you're not surprised when famous Christians get caught doing terrible things, your revulsion may stem from a particular church environment that turned you off from evangelicalism by the way someone close to you was treated. The dissonance you feel could also stem from how the evangelicals you know have (mis)handled subjects like science, sexuality, singleness, or supernatural gifts. Perhaps it's all of the above.

You're not alone.

My struggle with evangelicalism began shortly after I graduated from Wheaton College in 2003. During the presidential primary races of 2004, I worked as a news intern for WGN Radio in Chicago. That was the year George W. Bush ran for reelection. When I began my internship in January, the field of candidates vying to be Bush's Democratic challenger numbered about half a dozen. In addition to answering the newsroom phone (I never had to fetch coffee, strangely), one of my duties was curating sound bites from the campaign trail to be used during newscasts at the top of every hour. To gather these audio clips, I'd listen to live feeds of stump speeches and press conferences each day, choosing segments that captured a candidate's tone and content but with enough variety to avoid redundancy. Over the next few months, I became quite familiar with the speeches of John Kerry, John Edwards, Wesley Clark, Howard Dean, Al Sharpton, and of course, President Bush.

Crafting news copy around those speeches not only put me in touch with the American political scene at that time, it also sparked an interest in how faith and politics shape each other. Bush's reelection victory reflected the Religious Right's influence within evangelicalism, and by comparison, the Religious Left's lack thereof. This disparity troubled me, so I began asking questions about why so many evangelicals supported funding for the occupation of Iraq and the torture of enemy prisoners using methods like waterboarding but opposed funding for food stamps, public education, and medical care.

In 2005, I read Jim Wallis's book, *God's Politics: Why the Right Gets It Wrong and the Left Doesn't Get It*, which gave voice to the disconnect I felt between the Religious Right's brand of Christianity and the teachings of Jesus. Wallis further piqued my interest when he told Jon Stewart the following on *The Daily Show*:

> We need a better conversation about moral values. Are there only two: abortion and gay marriage? I'm an evangelical Christian. . . . I would say that fighting poverty is a moral value. I'd say protecting the environment, God's creation, is a moral value. I'd say how and when we go to war—and whether we tell the truth about it—is a moral value. Is torture a moral value? Let's have a better conversation about this.[1]

From there, I started reading *Sojourners*, the magazine Wallis founded, alongside *Christianity Today, The Economist, Relevant,* and the late *Books & Culture,* rest its soul. Up next was Shane Claiborne's 2006 book *The Irresistible Revolution,* followed by Greg Boyd's *The Myth of a Christian Nation: How the Quest for Political Power Is Destroying the Church* in 2007. In early 2008, I started a blog to process my thoughts on everything from gender roles and pop culture to presidential politics (it was primary season again) and theological trends within evangelicalism, like the growing rift between New Calvinism and the Emerging Church.

Did I mention my blog was eclectic? The first twenty posts included a book review, a music review, a piece about calls to boycott the Beijing Olympics, a five-thousand-word analysis of Honolulu's proposed rail transit project, and a thirty-nine-word poem with each line shorter than the last—resulting in the shape of an upside-down triangle. I also wrote an hour-by-hour recap of my first day in grad school, a reflection on the deadly sin of envy, two posts about basketball (college and pro, respectively), and one each on evangelism, Earth Day, capital punishment, and the doctrine of common grace.[2]

Speaking of common grace, it was through the exploration of these eclectic interests that my appreciation grew for the writings and public voice of Richard Mouw, who was then Fuller Seminary's president. I was especially drawn to the astounding ease with which Mouw could find theological common ground with almost anyone, not in spite of his Calvinist convictions but *because* of them. I had first heard him speak when he gave the 2003 commencement address to my graduating class at Wheaton. A couple years later, while browsing the shelves at Honolulu's Logos Bookstore, I stumbled upon his little book *Calvinism in the Las Vegas Airport*. It was such an unexpectedly enjoyable and compelling read that I devoured it in a couple sittings. Shattering my stereotypes of Calvinism as a rigid, Puritanical system committed to preserving male authority, Mouw introduced me to the world of his favorite theologian, Abraham Kuyper, also a fervent Calvinist but one whose seemingly strongest point of overlap with John Piper was that their last names rhymed. Everything else between Kuyper and Piper was a case in contrasts, not only in tone and focus but also politics and cultural engagement. Apparently Calvinists don't all agree! Dating back to my undergrad days at Wheaton a few years prior, I had until then assumed that Piper's interpretation of Calvinism was authoritative and uncontested. And yet in Mouw's Kuyperian version of Calvinism, women could be pastors, wars could be protested, and through the idea of common grace, the scope of God's care extended to all areas of creation and society, creating the basis for redemptive collaboration across any number of differences.

After hearing Mouw speak at the Hawaiian Islands Ministries conference in 2006 on "How to be a Public Christian," I found myself reading as much of his work as possible, from columns on Beliefnet.com to his Fuller blog, *Mouw's Musings*. When I started blogging in 2008, I was reading *He Shines in All That's Fair*, Mouw's lectures on culture and common grace, titled after a phrase in the hymn, "This Is My Father's World." At last, here was a Calvinist who valued both God's sovereignty and social action! As my Kuyperian horizons broadened, I discovered magazines like *Comment* and think tanks like The Center for Public Justice. It's no coincidence that after finishing my social work degree in 2011, I promptly started online classes at Fuller Seminary, in large part due to Mouw's effect on me.

As my seminary years began, I remained interested in conversations around the church's role in public life. Thus began my struggle to navigate the dissonance between who evangelicals purport to be as followers of Jesus, and who evangelicals are when capitulating to idolatries like Christian nationalism and injustices like white supremacy. Where was my place in all of this? Was it more problematic to identify as an evangelical or not? My time working in that election year newsroom may have started the ball rolling, but I soon realized that the struggle went deeper than candidates, campaigns, and cable news. Even if we could remove partisan politics from the equation, evangelical Christianity has supplied ample cause for mixed feelings about this particular expression of faith.

Blogging about evangelicalism helped clarify some of my ambivalence. At the same time, it stoked a stronger curiosity to find out why this topic mattered so much to me and a deeper longing to make sense of the mess. Entering my thirties stirred up new questions: How many possible meanings does *evangelical* have and how do we distinguish between them? If this label causes such a reactionary ruckus, why can't we seem to stop using it? When we get pulled into the cycle of debating the word's usefulness and proper usage, what effect does that have on our capacity for constructive conversation about cultivating a healthier evangelicalism, without minimizing either its brokenness or beauty?

I was initially dismayed to learn that Mouw's time as Fuller's president was ending in 2013, the year before Rebecca and I planned on moving our family from Honolulu to Pasadena so that we could both be full-time seminarians. However, shortly after we arrived there in 2014, I was delighted to discover through his fabulous assistant, Tammi (who just so happened to be my pre-assigned vocational formation small group facilitator during my first quarter on campus), that since Mouw's schedule was no longer packed with running the seminary, he now had more time to connect with students! Almost immediately, I gathered some classmates from the MDiv program and set about forming a "Kuyper Club" in the hopes of enticing Mouw to meet with us on a regular basis. Thanks to Tammi's influence, we made it onto his calendar, and our little reading group had a blast getting to know Dr. Mouw in person over the next several years, eventually reaching the outer orbit of those who call him "Rich." Living in seminary housing surrounded by classmates from around the world, I learned that Fuller is neither shy about identifying itself as an evangelical institution nor reluctant to name and address evangelicalism's shortcomings. This willingness to engage gray areas was part of what drew us there.

In 2015, Fuller's magazine devoted an entire issue to a one-word theme: *Evangelical*.[3] That issue served up a feast's worth of food for thought from a diverse cross-section of scholars and practitioners. I read it from cover to cover, but one article stayed with me, "Confessions of a Reluctant Evangelical," in which theology professor Dr. Erin Dufault-Hunter describes her struggle with both the label and the entity to which it points. She confesses that she often wants "to be cool more than I want to be Christian" yet chooses to claim and be claimed by evangelicalism because "I need my crazy kin. Just as I did not choose my blood family, I did not decide who would also come into this space of open gifts of grace and peace through Christ. . . . Despite our sometimes tense and important divergences, we are all claimed by the good news of what God has done in Christ, enticed by what God reveals in Scripture, and invigorated by the Spirit for engagement with a creation beloved by the One who created it."[4]

By articulating her struggle with evangelicalism, Dr. Erin, as students affectionately call her, had put her finger on something I hadn't yet realized about my own struggle: I wanted evangelicalism to claim me. I wanted to belong. Well, at least that's how I felt for an hour until the next time evangelicalism did something irksome (sigh).

Still, that article marked a tipping point. I began tracing the struggle back to a desire for belonging. I wanted to fit somewhere, not just in Christianity (too big) or my church's denomination (too small) but tethered to evangelicalism as an interdenominational, multiethnic space distinct enough to be its own faith stream yet broad enough to include a range of role models and kindred spirits. The struggle was far from over, but I began approaching it differently. I could no longer look the other way and remain at peace. It was time to face the quandary. And if Dr. Erin's reluctance persisted after many years of discipleship and deep reflection, perhaps mine would too.

By the end of 2015, I had started a Google document compiling links to articles about evangelicalism that resonated with me. I wasn't trying to write a book at that point. I just wanted to find patterns that might help make sense of my confusion. Amazed by how much was being written about the label's baggage alone, I separated the articles that grappled with the label from those that did not. That's when I began noting contrasts between what I now call the brand and the space. If an article was insightful, I'd summarize it and make note of key themes. Even in a non-election year, it felt like evangelicalism was making news every day, with opinions swirling from every direction. So many articles came across my radar that I only had time to save the links, hoping to read them later.

By the time I graduated from Fuller in mid-2016, presidential campaign season was in full swing, complete with the usual attention given to white evangelical voters' preferences. Coverage of non-white evangelicals was scant at best, if mentioned at all. Donald Trump surprised many pundits by securing the

Republican Party's nomination, even as his Democratic opponent Hillary Clinton appeared to be leading in most polls. Trump's supporters would prove those polls wrong, electing him as America's forty-fifth president.

In January 2017, I attended InterVarsity's national staff conference in Orlando. While there, I saw an announcement for a meet-up with IVP staff to learn about writing opportunities; I decided to go. By that point, I was considering writing a book about evangelicalism but wanted to learn more about IVP's proposal process. The staff were very informative, and I left the meeting with a sense that I needed to develop my ideas by writing something shorter first.

Over the next year, I continued working on that Google doc, compiling articles and making notes on how the evangelical brand differs and overlaps with evangelicalism as a space. As the election's anniversary approached that fall, an opportunity arose to write for Missio Alliance, thanks to an unexpected coffee meeting in Pasadena with Missio's then-director, JR Rozko. Missio Alliance is a parachurch network that organizes conferences and online content, providing theological and practical direction for North American church leaders in the vein of the Lausanne movement.[5] Its resources have been a breath of fresh air for evangelicals seeking an alternative to "New Calvinist" complementarian networks like The Gospel Coalition and the Acts 29 Network.[6] JR liked my contrast between brand and space, so I worked on an article that was eventually published in January 2018, one year after President Trump's inauguration.

Part of me was hoping that writing an article or two would get the topic out of my system so that I wouldn't have to continue contemplating whether or not to attempt a book proposal. As

2018 unfolded, however, it became clear that even if the proposal wasn't accepted, I felt a sense of urgency to at least follow through. If it was rejected, I would know I tried. But if it was accepted, it would be worth putting my struggle into words to help someone else find hope.

Our family moved from Southern California back home to Honolulu that fall, which delayed things a bit, but in February 2019 I finally submitted the proposal. It had been over two years since Orlando, four years since reading Dr. Erin's article, eleven years since starting a blog, and fifteen years since my internship in a radio newsroom. Did I mention this was just the proposal? Even after its acceptance, my struggle with evangelicalism persisted.

Why tell you this if it won't eliminate the struggle? The short answer is that struggles are not all created equal. Your journey might look very different from mine. You might not find any appeal in claiming or being claimed by evangelicalism. My goal isn't for you to land in the same place as me, Dr. Erin, or anyone else mentioned in these pages. This book is less of a roadmap and more of a compass. If you've ever grappled with mixed emotions about evangelicalism, this book is for you. If you're repulsed by the brand yet still inhabit evangelical spaces, this book will help you navigate the dissonance. If you're puzzled by how evangelicalism can be so broken yet beautiful at the same time, we'll unpack the reasons together.

AWKWARD SACRAMENTS

Evangelicalism is far from monolithic because it encompasses so many denominations and traditions, yet its variety of expression contains a distinct flavor. Take the practice of Communion for example. Between the type of bread, form of distribution, and style of musical accompaniment, evangelicals celebrate the Lord's Supper in many ways. Sometimes the congregation remains seated while trays are passed down each row. At other times, most people rise and form a line near the front.

There's also the question of music. A group of instrumentalists, often called a worship team or praise band, might play softly as the elements are distributed, or the process can be accompanied by prerecorded music. Sometimes evangelicals pre-cut the Communion bread, but at other times they practice intinction (colloquially known as "rip and dip"). Some churches use crushed crackers; some distribute paper-thin wafers. Once served, the elements might be held in hand until all partake together. At other times, congregants eat in turn as they head back to their seats.

Since evangelicals tend to emphasize personal faith, church services are designed facilitate an individual encounter with God. A worship team of musicians helps create an atmosphere conducive to such encounters. Sometimes the goal of a personalized encounter conflicts with the goal of sharing the experience as a group. Clashing priorities can produce awkward results. In order to set a worshipful tone, the band might play a song while Communion elements are served. If this is not carefully planned in advance, musicians can find themselves in a situation where their hands are needed for two different actions at once: receiving Communion and playing their instrument. Without a suitable surface upon which to set down their bread (unsanitary without a plate) and cup (risking stains if spilled), a dilemma arises for each instrumentalist.

Option A: Attempt to continue playing while consuming the bread and juice. This risks a potentially distracting musical hiccup and a couple awkwardly rushed movements from hand to mouth, especially with the juice. Option B: Cease playing the instrument for a longer period of time in order to reverently hold the elements securely in hand. This risks unintended musical consequences if the band relies on that instrument's part to carry the song. Most pianos and keyboards have a flat surface within reach and wide enough for an individual Communion cup, but guitarists, drummers, and bass players don't typically enjoy this luxury. Without sufficient guidance or preplanning, each musician must decide which to prioritize: playing their instrument or receiving the elements in hand.

I recall one particular Communion Sunday when this scenario played out unceremoniously at first. The music sounded great, but when it came time for the band members to be served Communion, a noticeable change occurred. As each instrumentalist paused to receive the bread and cup, the sound mix changed as if their instrument had been unexpectedly muted. First, the guitar dropped out, then returned once the guitarist had partaken. Next, the piano dropped out for the same reason, then returned. The drums ceased briefly but came back, followed by the bass. As each instrument briefly paused, the song kept going, but our ears were treated to a unique arrangement, the likes of which we've never heard before and would be rather difficult to replicate!

I suspect these awkwardly holy moments aren't uncommon in evangelical worship spaces featuring a worship band tasked with playing accompaniment during Communion. Even if unintended, the rotation of instruments being silent reflects the trajectory of 1 Corinthians 12:12: "Just as a body, though one, has many parts, but all its many parts form one body, so it is with

Christ." There's beauty in the sequence of taking turns, especially given the theological significance of pausing one's routine to cradle the body and blood of Christ, broken and shed for us. It reminds us why we're gathered for music-making in the first place.

Having said that, this scene would be unlikely without a peculiar recipe of evangelical-flavored ingredients: music designed for a personal encounter with God combined with the communal action of sharing the Lord's Table as God's family. Which priority takes precedence? I've often faced this dilemma in my experience leading worship teams. It's tough for instrumentalists to choose between two essential tasks when their hands can only perform one at a time. Which role takes precedence: parishioner or musician? It sounds strange to describe the dilemma that way but makes perfect sense within an evangelical context that values both personal encounter and group participation.

In addition to the beauty of taking turns, this scene also reveals a bit of sacramental clumsiness on the part of well-intentioned evangelicals. While I can appreciate blending tradition with innovation, it can come off like the two are at odds, as if the Eucharist celebration is interrupting our regularly scheduled rock music. How ironic to rehearse our songs thoroughly enough to anticipate every chord change and vocal harmony yet not give commensurate attention to how the precious symbols of Christ's body and blood will be partaken to nourish us as God's people.

Perhaps it's very evangelical of me to even consider a musical hiccup such a problem in the first place! Surely the gifts from the Lord's Table are worth far more than any worship we could bring. Indeed, evangelicalism is beautiful and broken, awkward sacraments and all. But it makes me feel at home.

GRAPPLING REALISTICALLY AND REDEMPTIVELY

Coastal cliffs are a mixed bag, offering breathtaking views but also hazardous landslides. In a similar way, evangelicalism can be simultaneously life-giving and dangerous. Much of the recent commotion surrounding the evangelical label reacts to one of these seemingly incompatible characteristics. On one hand, cynicism has swelled because hypocrisy, injustice, and abuse repeatedly harm those Jesus commanded us to love. Cynicism's negative filter makes it increasingly difficult for some to see any hope for evangelicalism's future. At the spectrum's other end, conversations tend to focus on evangelicalism in its ideal form, emphasizing what it *should* or *could* be if we lived out our values faithfully or recaptured the best of our heritage. This idealistic approach sets a high bar with good intentions, but, like cynicism, it tells an incomplete story by failing to describe evangelicalism as it really is: a mixed bag.

This book proposes a third way that is neither idealistic nor cynical. In order to take the mixed bag seriously, I believe we can neither disavow evangelicalism on account of its brokenness nor minimize its complicity in ongoing patterns of idolatry and injustice. By grappling with a more realistic account of evangelicalism experienced from the inside, this book aims to cultivate appreciation for the gifts God has given us, even as we learn to repent for our collective sins. As we come to terms with a complicated space, we must neither yield to the status quo nor oversimplify the mess we're in.

Beginning in the next chapter, I'll suggest four active postures that are essential for grappling realistically and redemptively with evangelicalism. These postures are awareness, appreciation, repentance, and renewal. Without awareness, we're like the baby bird in *Are You My Mother?* Without appreciation, we risk succumbing to cynicism. Without repentance, we capitulate to idolatry and injustice. Without renewal, future generations of evangelicals will find this space even less inhabitable. For each posture, we'll spend one chapter exploring what it is and why it matters, then another chapter on how to cultivate it.

Until we engage evangelicalism's good and bad in an integrated way, we won't come to terms with our mixed feelings about this influential space where so many have encountered Jesus in direct and personal ways. Whether you're on the brink of leaving evangelicalism behind, strongly committed to staying, or somewhere in between, I desire to help you make an informed decision about your relationship with evangelicalism moving forward. Are you ready?

Part I

AWARENESS

2

DEFINING EVANGELICALISM

Understanding Our History

GEOGRAPHY CHANGES EVERYTHING. As a Hawai'i-born missionary kid growing up in Africa and Asia, my cultural sensibilities became attuned to the nuances of different locations. Food, clothing, and music in the Congo were vastly different from the Philippines. Norms varied from place to place, including rates of speech, hand gestures, and facial expressions. Standards of time, promptness, respect, and honor also differed. It all depended on my location. As a result, I'm wary of declarations that claim universality without an awareness of one's own location. Some cultures value happiness over success, whereas for other cultures it might be the opposite. For every parent in a Western society who longs for their children to develop self-confidence and find fulfillment as they follow their own path, there's a family elsewhere who longs for their children to learn the importance of cooperation, group harmony, and self-control.

Moving from country to country made it difficult to put down roots. Where was home? Where was I from? My passport certified me as a US citizen, but I didn't feel at home in the United States until well after college. It was a disorienting way to grow up, yet my US passport granted me tremendous privileges. If conditions deteriorated in one country, our family had the option of retreating to the United States to wait things out, as we did during Zaïre's civil war in the early 1990s. Our passports gave us the freedom to visit almost any country, with the option to utilize US embassy protection if we needed it. Living abroad was an optional endeavor, a risk-taking step of faith for my parents yet also a calculated choice if they felt that the benefits outweighed the risks. Most children my age in Zaïre, Nepal, and the Philippines did not have access to the resources I did. Given the economic and social conditions of these places, why did God allow me to be born in an air-conditioned hospital in Hawai'i cradled by loving parents who were not only married, Christian, and homeowning but both of whom had already received a graduate level education?

My upbringing exposed me to the powerful effect of geographic location on human experience, including one's experience of God. Evangelical churches in Nepal worship Jesus in a different style and with different assumptions than evangelical churches in the United States. Evangelical pastors in the Congo preach and teach from the Bible but with different emphases than evangelical pastors in the Philippines. As I realized the power of location to shape norms, assumptions, and ideas, I came to see evangelicalism less as a brand and more as a space. A brand is what one buys, but a space is where one lives. Switching brands might alter our budget or how we look; changing homes—especially moving from one culture to another—can affect every area of life as we've known it.

DEFINING EVANGELICALISM

The word *evangelical* comes from the Greek word *euangelion*, meaning "gospel" or "good news." In order to cultivate a healthier evangelicalism, we must first know what evangelicalism is. Even when we agree that *evangelicalism* is a reality to be reckoned with, the hard part is reaching a consensus on what exactly it is. Eleven months before the US presidential election of 2016, Jonathan Merritt wrote, "Technically speaking, *evangelical* refers to a person, church, or organization that is committed to the Christian gospel message that Jesus Christ is the savior of humanity."[1] While it sounds simple enough to define evangelicals as people committed to the gospel, this broad definition makes "evangelical" almost synonymous with "Christian." There is nothing wrong with thinking of evangelicals as Christians—I hope we are! But even if all evangelicals are Christians, it doesn't follow that all Christians are evangelicals. All penguins are birds, but not all birds are penguins. If we define Christians as people who are committed to the gospel message of Christ as humanity's Redeemer and Lord, there are plenty of Christians who aren't evangelicals—including those who belong to Catholic, Eastern Orthodox, and mainline Protestant church traditions. Following Jesus doesn't require membership in an evangelical church, or even a Protestant one. After all, three-quarters of church history took place before Protestant churches existed.

Tricky as it may be to define evangelicalism, let's give it a try. According to historian Kristin Kobes Du Mez, evangelicalism exists as four things at once: a theological category, a cultural movement, a white religious brand, and a diverse global movement.[2] Let's unpack each of those briefly, because Du Mez is onto something important here.

THEOLOGICAL CATEGORY

First, evangelicalism is a *theological category*. The most widely used definition in the past thirty years is the "Bebbington quadrilateral," which names four points of emphasis that characterize evangelicals:

1. Conversionism: the need to repent from sin and turn to Christ in faith

2. Biblicism: devotion to the Bible as inspired by God

3. Activism: dedication to share the Christian message, near and far

4. Crucicentrism: belief that Jesus' death on the cross reconciles us to God[3]

When evangelicalism is defined as a theological category, it functions as criteria to determine whether a person, church, or organization qualifies as evangelical or not. To use the title of historian Thomas Kidd's book as an example, the question becomes, "Who is an evangelical?"

According to Kidd, "Evangelicals are born-again Protestants who cherish the Bible as the Word of God and who emphasize a personal relationship with Jesus through the Holy Spirit."[4] Kidd's definition includes three components:

1. Conversion: Protestants who are born-again

2. Bible: Scripture is cherished as God's Word

3. Divine presence: a personal relationship with Jesus through
   the Spirit

Notice how the first two are also found on Bebbington's list,
but Kidd makes "divine presence" the third pillar instead of activism and crucicentrism. Without denying activism or crucicentrism, he instead highlights evangelicals' emphasis on having "a
personal relationship with Jesus through the Holy Spirit." Evangelicals aren't the only Christians who value this, yet it would be
hard to find an evangelical church or organization whose
members don't understand their relationship with Jesus as
something personal whereby God's nearness can be intimately
experienced through the Holy Spirit.

One example of how *evangelical* functions as a theological
category can be seen in some of the pushback against the now
infamous statistic of 81 percent of white evangelicals voting for
presidential candidate Donald Trump in 2016.[5] What does this
statistic mean? Technically, it means that 81 percent of the white
voters who self-identified as evangelicals cast a vote for Mr. Trump,
a number that would dip slightly to 76 percent in the 2020 election.[6] Critics who question these high percentages point to the
fact that theological criteria aren't used to define "evangelical" in
exit polls. According to Lifeway Research, less than half of the
Americans who identify as evangelical hold evangelical beliefs,
and one-third of the Americans who hold evangelical views don't
identify as evangelical.[7] Therefore, the argument goes, a sizable
chunk of the 81 percent should not be considered true evangelicals because their beliefs don't fit the theological category.
Moreover, critics point out that some evangelicals were not captured by this data, despite meeting the theological criteria, because they don't self-identify with the evangelical label.

Does this critique have merit? Yes and no. Although it's possible that the 81 percent figure might have been lower had theological criteria been used instead of self-identification, it should be noted that, for better or worse, self-identification is the water in which these exit polls swim. Theological criteria aren't used for counting Catholic or Black Protestant voters either. Regardless of how much distance we'd like to put between ourselves and the 81 percent, the fact remains that this demographic voted in higher numbers for Donald Trump than the three previous Republican presidential candidates: Mitt Romney in 2012 (79%), John McCain in 2008 (73%), and George W. Bush in 2004 (79%).[8] Even Jimmy Carter, a Southern Baptist and self-described "born-again Christian," won the presidency in 1976 with support from only 47 percent of white voters and 44 percent of Protestant voters.[9] Newsweek magazine ran a cover story that dubbed 1976 the "Year of the Evangelicals" because of how Carter's campaign drew theologically conservative Christians from the margins of political engagement back into the mainstream.[10]

CULTURAL MOVEMENT

If evangelicalism were just a theological category, it would be much easier to define. We wouldn't need to explore how it functions as a space where, over time, shared habits and tendencies become customs, even traditions. I've heard it said that evangelicals don't have traditions, but that's false. Praying extemporaneous (unscripted) prayers and singing screen-projected lyrics are examples of deeply ingrained evangelical rituals, practiced with the same regularity as baseball fans singing "Take Me Out to the Ball Game" during the seventh-inning stretch.

This brings us to the second thing Du Mez says evangelicalism is: a *cultural movement*. According to Wheaton College's former Institute for the Study of American Evangelicals (since closed), this sense of the term denotes "a style as much as a set of beliefs, and an attitude which insiders know and feel when they encounter it."[11] If evangelicalism were a style of cuisine, it would have a distinct blend of flavors. Anthropologist Tanya Luhrmann writes, "The feature that most deeply characterizes [evangelicals] is that the God they seek is more personally intimate, and more intimately experienced, than the God most Americans grew up with."[12]

What kind of place is it? Evangelicalism is where a generation of kids learned the song "Lean on Me" from DC Talk in the early 1990s, instead of the original by Bill Withers that was a number one hit in the early 1970s. It's where the tune of "Louie, Louie" is better known as "Pharaoh, Pharaoh." It's where phrases like "True Love Waits" and "See You at the Pole" take us back in time. If you're too young (or too old) to have experienced evangelical youth group culture in the 1990s, feel free to ignore these examples. The point remains: evangelicalism doesn't just foster shared beliefs, it creates shared experiences that make it identifiable as a distinct culture with its own melodies and vocabulary. That's why so many evangelicals know what it means to *stand in the gap*, be *on fire for God*, and pray for *a hedge of protection*. And if you don't know how to do *popcorn prayers*, share *praise reports*, or *love on people*, you'll be fine if you keep *pressing in*. Just *let go and let God*.

WHITE RELIGIOUS BRAND

Third, evangelicalism is a *white religious brand*. You can't understand evangelicalism without tracing the influence of race on how it operates. There's a reason why polls use the categories of "white evangelical" and "Black protestant" as mutually exclusive. When polls use the label, the only evangelicals who get counted are white. Why is this word not attached to any other racial group? Why is "Asian evangelical" not an option?

It's also understandable why there may be a reluctance among Black Christians to use the term. A twitter thread from Jemar Tisby explains the factors in play:

> I know the phrase "Black evangelical" makes sense from a certain perspective—what else do you call a Black Christian who is in evangelical circles? It's also convenient shorthand because there may not be another easily accessible descriptor. BUT . . . // Many Black Christians explicitly reject the label "evangelical." Sometimes people don't realize they are part of a group or reject a label even as their actions identify them with it. But it's also true that actors' terms and how people self-identify are important. // In my view, "Black evangelical" is a historically rooted term that comes to the fore in the mid-20th century as white evangelicals invite Black Christians into their organizations and institutions (colleges, Bible institutes, campus ministries) in token numbers. // From about the 1950s-1990s there was a generation of Black Christian who self-identified as Black evangelicals. Even in this, however, they felt it necessary to say "Black" and evangelical—it acknowledges their marginalization in white evangelical spaces. // Anecdotally, I don't know any Black Christians under the age of 40 (maybe even 50?) who use the term Black evangelical to describe themselves. They may say that a belief or a movement or a church is evangelical, but they don't call

themselves that. // I usually see Black Christians, especially those in predominantly white evangelical spaces, explicitly rejecting the term "evangelical" (some white folks do as well). I often say that such Black Christians are "evangelical-adjacent." The proximity to white Christians is important // So what terms do you use instead of "Black evangelical"? Some say "Bible-believing" Christian. Others say their denominational affiliation (COGIC, AME, Baptist, etc.). I simply say "Black Christian."[13]

Amid all the attention given to white evangelicals, it's notable that one-third of American evangelicals are people of color, including nearly half of evangelicals under age thirty.[14] Twenty-two percent of young evangelical Protestants are Black, 18 percent are Hispanic, and 9 percent identify as some other race or mixed race. Only 50 percent of evangelical Protestants under the age of thirty are white, compared to more than three-quarters (77%) of evangelical Protestant seniors (age 65 or older).[15]

Here's the point: Christianity is far bigger and more diverse than evangelicalism's brand name version. Less than 3 percent of the world's evangelicals are white Americans. Less than 3 percent! As someone who spent ten years of his childhood outside the United States, you'd think I would know this. Yet I still slip into assuming that white Americans constitute the center of evangelicalism. This only underscores further why awareness is critical as we locate ourselves on Christianity's big map.

DIVERSE GLOBAL MOVEMENT

Du Mez's fourth way of understanding evangelicalism is a *diverse global movement*. Depending on the term's definition, evangelicals make up somewhere between 16 and 29 percent of the US population.[16] Even if we estimated on the high end (29%), this translates to 97.5 million evangelicals in a US population of 330 million people. At first glance, 97.5 million might seem like a big number, but that's only 18 percent of the world's 545.9 million evangelicals according to Operation World.[17] It might surprise some American Christians that 82 percent of the world's evangelicals live outside the United States.

When accounting for Catholics, mainline Protestants, and Eastern Orthodox believers, we see that Christianity is much bigger than evangelicalism. The Pew Research Center estimates the global population of Christians at 2.4 billion.[18] If we use Operation World's estimate of 545.9 million global evangelicals, it means less than one fourth (23%) of the world's Christians are evangelicals. Based on these numbers, American evangelicals are just 4 percent of the global body of Christ (see figure 2.1).[19]

In her book, *The Kingdom of God Has No Borders*, Melani McAlister posits that much can be learned about American

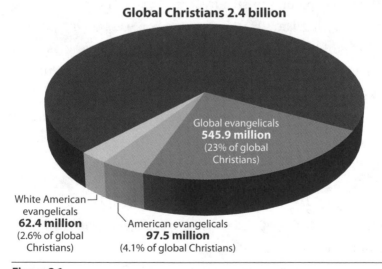

Global Christians 2.4 billion

Global evangelicals
545.9 million
(23% of global Christians)

White American
evangelicals
62.4 million
(2.6% of global Christians)

American evangelicals
97.5 million
(4.1% of global Christians)

Figure 2.1

evangelicals from what they do outside the United States, including short-term mission trips. She writes about how contemporary Christian music has helped develop the vision of the short-term traveler. To make their 2004 album, *Share the Well,* the band Caedmon's Call traveled to Ecuador, Brazil, and India, crafting songs about global poverty, non-American Christianity, and social justice. McAlister points to *Share the Well* as unique "precisely because the level of evangelical self-awareness is so low."[20] The album is an exception to the prevailing view of short-term missions (epitomized by songs like Audio Adrenaline's "Hands and Feet"), which can exoticize an overseas set of enchanted experiences. By contrast, Caedmon's Call's song "Mother India" communicates that "the American singer does not bring God's grace to India; God's reach begins there and brings her in."[21]

A WORKING DEFINITION

So which definition is correct? It turns out that there is not one evangelicalism but many evangelicalisms. Du Mez describes these as four overlapping entities that are all identified with the same term. No matter how much we distance ourselves from any of the four, we can't seem to stop using the e-word. After all, it's a term that means at least four things! Without an awareness of all four, our picture is incomplete. It's a theological category, yes, but also a subculture, a white religious brand, and a global movement.

This book's approach views evangelicalism as a space, a spiritual habitat where over half a billion Christians live out their faith. The term can refer to religious and political phenomena within white America or a theological subset of Christians within Protestantism, but those definitions don't capture all that evangelicalism is. As helpful as each definition may be, it paints only part of the picture. The theological category is an important feature of the space, as is the white religious brand, but I see evangelicalism primarily as the space itself, the zipcode of our spiritual lives. It's where we're located on the big map of Christianity. We don't have to identify with the evangelical brand to live here any more than we have to identify with the bald eagle, Uncle Sam, and Lady Liberty to inhabit the United States. Like any neighborhood, there are pros and cons to living here. Like any habitat, it can be a healthy place to flourish or a toxic place that drains the life from us.

With all due respect to Bebbington, there are other Christian streams that value conversion, Scripture, Christ's atonement, and evangelism. We aren't the only ones who care about saving souls, trusting the Bible, focusing on the cross, and joining God's mission. What makes evangelicalism unique is the particular way we go about it. More importantly, I would argue, evangelicalism is the place *where* we go about it. If your spiritual home is located here, you're an evangelical as far as I'm concerned.

HOW WE GOT HERE

Of Du Mez's four definitions, the third one receives the most media attention: a white religious brand that functions as a voting bloc. For many Americans, the e-word is inextricably political. As a result, people who fit one of the other three definitions but disagree politically with the Christian Right are apt to drop the label. I find this understandable and have felt similar inclinations at times. In an era when self-identifying along religious or political lines makes a strong social statement, I can see why the term has fallen out of favor. At the same time, it's important to know how we got into this conundrum to begin with.

While digging deeper into the history of this term's usage over the past few centuries, I discovered that *evangelical* hasn't always carried this much political baggage. Things were different in the late 1800s, when being evangelical meant living out a passion for Jesus in ways that did not isolate personal piety from social justice. These evangelicals were just as passionate about addressing social ills as they were about saving souls. As Jim Wallis has said, "I'm a nineteenth-century evangelical, born in the wrong century. Because back then, Charles Finney, Lucy Stone, the Grimke sisters, Jonathan Blanchard—these preachers, revivalists were also abolitionists. They led the antislavery campaign. They fought for women's suffrage. They fought for economic justice. In fact, Charles Finney, who was the evangelist, the Billy Graham of his day, really pioneered the altar call. And the reason he did was he wanted to sign his converts up for the antislavery campaign. So faith got directed right to justice."[22]

White evangelicals didn't become a sizable political voting bloc until the 1980s. They weren't always so focused on opposing abortion and same-sex marriage. On the other hand, there's nothing new about the word's meaning being contested and debated. According to historian George Marsden, it was actually the fundamentalists who initially wanted to abandon the label in the late 1970s.[23] The term's popularity has ebbed and flowed over the years. Apparently, the very act of debating what it means to be evangelical is a very evangelical thing to do!

Given how powerful the evangelical brand has become, it can be difficult to see things any other way. But if we want a reimagined approach that offers a more complete picture of what evangelicalism is, we need to understand the differences between the brand and the space. Both aspects are real and must be dealt with. For now, I'd like to suggest four ways that the evangelical brand differs from the evangelical space.

POLITICS VERSUS RELIGION

First, the evangelical brand is primarily about agendas that use religion for electoral gain, whereas the evangelical space is a religious locale manifesting itself in various ways, including politically but also economically and socioculturally. For example, evangelical dollars fund the contemporary Christian music industry, which, although generally conservative, has a primarily economic rather than political function. In the area of humanitarian work, evangelicals have been very engaged on the issue of sex trafficking, not because of a partisan platform but because of a desire to influence the world in accordance with their religious convictions.

WHITE AMERICAN VERSUS
MULTIRACIAL AND GLOBAL

Second, the evangelical brand is depicted almost exclusively as white American, which obfuscates evangelicalism's racial diversity and global multiculturalism. One-third of US evangelicals are people of color, but we wouldn't know it from the talking heads purported to speak for the evangelical brand. Americans make up less than 20 percent of evangelicals worldwide, but we wouldn't know it from most evangelicals' bookshelves or podcast feeds. Part of the problem stems from using the labels "evangelical" and "white American evangelical" interchangeably. When we describe the characteristics of white American evangelicalism without specifying that we're only referring to part of it, we send a message that collapses the whole into a smaller slice, which truncates aspects of the group that don't fit the brand. This becomes a myth-reinforcing system, whereby examples of evangelicalism that don't fit the white American brand are removed from the equation.

As a fourteen-year-old missionary kid living in Kathmandu, Nepal, I attended an international Christian school that operated on the British academic system. Instead of calling it middle school or eighth grade, I was in "class three." A few classmates had a US passport like mine, but most were from other countries: New Zealand, Canada, England, Pakistan, India, Germany, Northern Ireland, and the Maldives, to name a few. Most of them came from Protestant Christian families who were generally like-minded about following Jesus and studying the Bible but were not white American Republicans in the least. When America's election coverage industry mentions evangelical voters, they describe a sample size that doesn't include my international classmates and their families; the evangelical brand doesn't account for them.

CONSUMERS VERSUS INHABITANTS

Third, there's a major difference between the evangelical brand as something to consume versus a space to inhabit. With the rise of influential megachurches in the 1980s, such as Willow Creek and Saddleback Community Church, came a shift toward "seeker sensitive" ministry approaches intended to attract newcomers. As pews became theater seats, unchurched people were viewed as spiritual consumers. Services included a casual dress code, multimedia presentations, minimal audience participation, and short, practical sermons.

Missiologist Donald McGavran's *homogeneous unit principle*, developed at Fuller Seminary, played a major role in reshaping expectations of what church should be: attractive, large, and easy to join with as few cultural barriers as possible. His magnum opus, *Understanding Church Growth*, was voted by *Christianity Today* as the second most influential book in the twentieth century. In it, McGavran states that people "like to become Christians without crossing racial, linguistic or class barriers."[24]

For evangelicalism to be consumed individually, it needs all the trappings of a strong brand: compelling to the marketplace, attractive to buyers, trusted by consumers to scratch where they itch. To approach evangelicalism as a brand means browsing its shelves for something to wear. When my teenage son shops online for shoes, he's not just looking for what fits his feet. He wants a shoe whose brand expresses a message that fits his identity. While shopping alone in a physical store, I once found a great deal on sneakers his size that I brought home, only to discover that the brand apparently clashed with his group of friends at school. Consumer preferences and social circles can be hard to satisfy. In order to be strong and viable, a brand must match our tastes perfectly. This is how some treat the evangelical brand. If it doesn't enhance our appearance, express our identity, or at the very least make life easier instead of harder, we have no use for it. Conversely, if it substantially worsens our appearance or clashes with our identity, what are we waiting for? Evangelicalism must go!

Of the five countries where I've lived, there is none more consumeristic or brand-conscious than the United States. Advertisers beckon us to not only select the brand that's right for us but also stick with it as a matter of loyalty and self-expression. As a result, we drink this coffee but not that coffee. We'll drive this car but not that car. We'll use this phone but not that one. Every product comes with a logo and a slogan asserting its brand. The American Psychological Association estimates that advertisers spend over $12 billion per year to reach the youth market and that children view more than forty thousand commercials each year.[25] In a context like this, our religions and spiritual preferences have been branded too. When it's unflattering to identify as Christian, religious, or born-again, we rebrand as persons of faith or followers of Christ. Even so, religious and spiritual branding can only take us so far. We need another metaphor.

INDIVIDUAL VERSUS COLLECTIVE

An individual versus a collective mindset is the fourth way the evangelical brand differs from the space. On one hand, any attempt to define the label's scope will involve asking questions about individuals: Who is evangelical and who is not? Bebbington's quadrilateral can be helpful in this regard. On my quest to decide whether to identify as one or not, I've repeatedly asked myself: "Am I an evangelical? Do I meet the criteria?" These are important questions but also tend toward the brand-like assumption that centers the individual Christian as the primary unit of scrutiny. Does Dan Stringer meet the criteria or not? Does he identify as one or not?

When we approach evangelicalism as a space, our lens shifts from individual criteria to collective awareness. Instead of categorizing individuals, we begin asking questions about the boundaries and location of spaces. Take the example of California as a geographic place on the map. The question "Are you a Californian?" refers to one's individual status. Collective awareness isn't required to answer this question. All that's needed is an understanding of whether you meet the criteria. But answering the question "Is Fresno in California?" requires collective awareness of a geographic location. It requires an awareness of California less as a brand and more as a space. If you know where California ends and Nevada begins, you can answer the question about Fresno's location.

In a similar way, this book is concerned less with criteria for classifying individuals as evangelical and more with examining what kind of space evangelicalism is. What particular features mark its landscape? What are evangelicalism's strengths and weaknesses? How can we make evangelicalism more inhabitable for those who come after us? We'll focus less on categorizing individual Christians and more about understanding evangelicalism as an ecosystem and location on the map of Christianity. As far as this book is concerned, whether or not you're an individual evangelical matters less than whether evangelicalism is being left better or worse than how we found it.

3

FAITH STREAM AWARENESS

Knowing Your Location

AT SOME POINT IN MY MIDTWENTIES, I became fascinated by the world of church ministry strategy discussions. Things like the order of elements in a worship service, the style and goal of preaching, and the church's relationship to the neighborhood all interested me. The mid-2000s saw the emerging church movement pushing back against "attractional" megachurch models, as well as the move toward "missional" church approaches that sought to join God in the world rather than bring God to the world.

Around this same time, I was burned out on ministry from being too controlling as a worship leader in an older congregation that was experiencing a mild version of the "worship wars" between praise songs and hymns. During that time, I met a pastor from a different church who was about ten years older than me, eloquent, and sharp. I admired how culturally savvy he was about the latest trends in ministry and philosophy. When I asked if he would mentor me, he said yes. At least, I think that's what I asked for. Perhaps he just thought we were having coffee once a month or so.

In one of our conversations, he used a word that wasn't part of my vocabulary: *ecclesiology*. He said something like, "I wonder how many other people spend their Saturday mornings having coffee and talking about ecclesiology."

Was that what we were doing? Talking ecclesiology? It dawned on me that ecclesiology didn't have to be a dry and dusty doctrine on the shelf but something that I was already interested in. Some of my questions included: Why must our worship services and sermons be the way they are? Why can't we do more smells and bells and mystery and sacramental stuff like the high church folk do? Is there a way to flatten the church hierarchy so that it's less pyramid-shaped with a magnetic male at the top? We talked about church history and trends that have ebbed and flowed across the centuries. Connecting the dots between then and now, I began to see the tension between tradition and experience, between church growth and theological depth.

Later, I looked up the word "ecclesiology" to learn it comes from *ekklēsia*, the Greek word for church in the New Testament. Ecclesiology is the study of what the church is compositionally and theologically in relation to how it operates practically and missionally. Apparently these tensions are centuries old! And ecclesiology—I liked it. I lived and breathed it! Some have said that evangelicals don't have much of an ecclesiology. I would counter that we do, but it's more like a style of cuisine in which many different dishes are cooked a certain way to emphasize certain flavors. In due time I would write blog posts trying to sift through the various up-and-coming leaders who disagreed with each other about how to do church in postmodern contexts. I appreciated the merits of multiple viewpoints even as I started to form my own convictions on questions like the atonement and gender hierarchy.

Even without being enrolled in any school, it was an intellectually exciting time. I took copious notes at every church ministry conference or seminar I could attend, noting patterns and contrasts as bloggers debated what the Bible prescribed regarding church structures and theological priorities. Slowly but surely, I learned the differences between the various denominations I had been a part of—there were so many! I started talking with my wife, Rebecca, about where we might like to land ecclesiologically and theologically as we followed God's will together in ministry. The ecclesiology conversation had begun. A decade and half later, this book culminates that journey of grappling with my relationship to evangelicalism . . . so far.

INTRODUCING FAITH STREAM AWARENESS

On the journey toward a healthier evangelicalism, one starting point involves developing what I'm calling *faith stream awareness*. I define it as "the capacity to locate oneself as part of a particular stream or tradition within the broader Christian faith." A *faith stream* or *faith tradition* (I use the terms interchangeably here) is the subset of Christianity in which one practices their faith. Examples of Protestant faith streams include broader traditions (Methodist, Baptist, Pentecostal) as well as specific denominations (Assemblies of God, Southern Baptist Convention, Christian Reformed Church) or church networks (Calvary Chapel, Every

Nation, Willow Creek Association). Faith traditions are not limited to denominations or church networks. For some non-denominational or independent churches, identifiers like "Bible Church" or "Full Gospel" signify theological distinctives and ministry emphases. Thus, for Christians, faith stream awareness refers to your capacity to identify and be aware of the particular tradition(s) that have provided a context for your relationship with God and discipleship to Jesus.

Developing faith stream awareness is more about tracing your genealogy than knowing your personal preferences. It's about identifying the origins and influences on the space you now inhabit. While it's important to eventually determine whether your views today align with the streams that formed you, the key question for faith stream awareness is, Which stream(s) have formed my faith? Think of it as learning your spiritual family tree.

What qualifies as a faith stream? Some streams' roots reach back centuries (Reformed, Anglican, Anabaptist), but not every stream feels like a tradition. Calvary Chapel may not identify itself as a tradition, but its size (1,700 churches)[1] and unique qualities distinguish it as a faith stream, or at the very least, a movement within evangelicalism. Innovative church franchises birthed from megachurches seem anything but traditional, yet their discernable history and distinct patterns are manifest in what gets emphasized.

Faith stream awareness requires a certain measure of taxonomic differentiation, that is, the ability to distinguish between categories and sub-categories of faith streams. Christianity consists of many faith streams, networks, denominations, and broad traditions like Catholicism, Protestantism, and the Eastern Orthodox Church. Although it's certainly distinct from other religions (Judaism, Islam, Buddhism), the body of Christ is more like a wide river, or even a lake or sea. Christians with faith stream awareness can identify not only which denomination or tradition their local church belongs to but also what distinguishes that particular faith stream when compared to other streams. Evangelicals with faith stream awareness will acknowledge that their context emphasizes Jesus, the Bible, and discipleship in a certain way. Other Christian traditions care about these things, too, but with a different approach than evangelicals take. The next chapter will reveal how to cultivate this kind of awareness.

BENEFITS OF FAITH STREAM AWARENESS

I once had a Twitter conversation with my friend the Reverend Lauren Grubaugh exploring the benefits of self-awareness on a collective spiritual level. I asked her what she thought was the greatest benefit of being self-aware of one's spiritual location and influences.

She replied, "I believe that awareness of geographic particularity allows one to be in a relationship with others in a way that embraces them in the fullness of their context. The totalizing tendencies of decontextual Christianity include a disregard for the people and cultures which form us. // The effect is a flattened view of others, where we see a person as an individual, cut off from community."[2]

Lauren is basically saying we should pay attention to how our location forms us, especially if we're part of a predominant majority. We can do a lot of damage when we operate under an assumption that our culture's way is the default, with everything else being a variation of it. But our vantage point is just that: a location from where we see everything else.

Every mapmaker must decide which direction is up. It doesn't have to be north! Cartographers also decide where each map begins and ends. Even on maps that appear to be drawn from above, the person doing the drawing is likely on the map somewhere. Remembering this helps us locate ourselves. Applying this to evangelicalism, we don't want to be like the baby bird who doesn't know its own mother.

In summary, these are the benefits of faith stream awareness:

- Honesty and accuracy that gives spiritual influences their proper due

- Increased capacity to understand and appreciate people's spiritual journeys more fully

- Reduced harm from one-size-fits-all approaches that dehumanize the different

- Deeper insight on how to change broken patterns and systems

EVANGELICALISM'S STRENGTHS
AND WEAKNESSES

Lesslie Newbigin said, "Every statement of the gospel in words is conditioned by the culture of which those words are a part, and every style of life that claims to embody the truth of the gospel is a culturally conditioned style of life. There can never be a culture-free gospel. Yet the gospel, which is from the beginning to the end embodied in culturally conditioned forms, calls into question all cultures, including the one in which it was originally embodied."[3]

According to Newbigin, the good news of Jesus is always mediated by the culture of those speaking it and hearing it. You can't communicate the gospel without culture any more than you can use words without language. The goal isn't to escape our culture but to be aware of how it shapes the way we understand our faith and live it out. It's not a matter of *if* you're on the map but *where* on the map you are.

Every location on the globe features pros and cons for its residents. Even in beautiful Hawai'i, the place I call home, we experience lethal hurricanes, outrageous housing costs, and stressful competition for economic resources. Conversely, even the hottest deserts provide great views of the stars, fewer traffic jams, more clean air, and greater appreciation for the value of water—not to mention less mold (so I've heard). Wherever you live, it's vital to be aware of what your surroundings offer—and what they don't. Don't expect to snowboard much in the tropics or snorkel frequently in the Rocky Mountains. Be realistic.

Let's apply this to evangelicalism as a spiritual home. There are pros and cons to living here. Evangelicalism excels in certain ways while failing miserably in others. The more you know about what to expect from this habitat, the better equipped you'll be to nourish your soul in evangelical spaces. As your awareness increases, so will your capacity to nurture a healthier evangelicalism for the sake of others. Not only will you find life-giving resources for your own spiritual life, you'll be empowered to help those who are struggling to spiritually thrive here.

I believe God is calling evangelicalism to own its baggage, accepting that we have failed in significant ways while still possessing something incredibly life-giving to offer. This book won't supply an exhaustive list of evangelicalism's pros and cons. Instead, I'll give examples to help you survey the landscape in your particular locale. My observations come from personal experience and people I've known during my four decades inhabiting various pockets of evangelicalism. By no means have I tasted every flavor of evangelicalism (thankfully), but I've observed and noted enough patterns to give a realistic account of its strengths and weaknesses as a space. Let's first become aware of what those are before taking action to make things better.

THE PROS

Let's begin with the positives. If evangelicalism wasn't doing anything right, it wouldn't be the spiritual home for half a billion Christians around the globe. There's something about it that helps people experience the life-changing power of Jesus. Evangelicalism is where I learned how to pray, how to give away money (evangelical lingo: "tithing"), how to serve the needy, and how to stand up to injustice. I still have much to learn about each of these skills (evangelical lingo: "spiritual disciplines"), but that perspective came from evangelicals too.

Why was evangelicalism so good to me? Did I just get lucky? It wasn't until after college that I connected the dots between my personal experience and evangelicalism's strengths in general. The positives mentioned here are outworkings of what I now understand to be the gifts that evangelicalism brings to the table. Evangelicals have a reputation for being closed-minded, yet my time at an evangelical college encouraged me to welcome life's biggest questions. Wheaton taught me how to apply Christian beliefs to academic study (evangelical lingo: "integration of faith and learning"). My professors modeled how to explore a variety of viewpoints on theological and scientific questions. Because of that, I am grateful for evangelicalism.

With the caveat that experiences may vary, here's my top-five list of evangelicalism's strengths:

1. Love for Scripture: Not only does evangelicalism hold Scripture in high regard, its inhabitants encounter the living God through studying the Bible for themselves. We love Scripture because it reveals a God who is love (1 John 4:8). The Bible doesn't just inspire us; it transforms us. We take time to study its meaning and apply it to real life. Evangelicals put great effort into fostering fluency in the Bible's content and know how to make the text come alive.

2. Access to an intimate experience of God's presence:[4] By stressing that Christian faith is about having a direct, personal encounter with God, evangelicalism makes spiritual growth tremendously accessible. God is at our fingertips around the clock. He does not require a priest, building, liturgy, or sacred day of the week. He can speak to us through the Bible at any time—or even without the Bible! He has a specific plan and purpose for every person. A theology promoting this kind of divine immediacy and directness is not only attractive and marketable, it has helped many people enter the Christian faith. That God wants a personal relationship with you is a simple and straightforward message that attaches no church strings, at least not right away. One can meet God and find salvation at a rock concert or in front of a laptop screen. In this ecclesiology, the church's role is to energize your personal relationship with God and keep your faith on track, but an individual's connection to God is what ultimately matters. American evangelicalism's emphasis on God's immediacy represents a tremendous evangelistic advantage because

it's always trying to shorten the distance between individuals and God.

3. Adaptivity for mission: By prioritizing individual faith and spiritual growth rather than adherence to tradition or denominational structures, evangelical churches are afforded a high degree of flexibility in developing their ministry operations. Consequently, this allows freedom to adapt to community needs or reassess church policies that seem ineffective. If a church wants to change its order of worship to be more intelligible, it can. If a church wants to explore the possibility of switching over to a denomination that supports the ordination of women, there are options. If a church wants to geographically relocate, change its name, or merge with another congregation in order to follow the Holy Spirit's leading, evangelicalism's ecclesiology makes it possible to do so. Adaptability to contextual shifts represents a great strength because it maximizes the church's freedom to reimagine new ways when the old ways are not working.

4. Ecumenical collaboration: Alongside its capacity for freedom and change, evangelical ecclesiology allows for opportunities to traverse denominational lines in service of causes that are deemed significant priorities. Vibrant interdenominational parachurch organizations represent one of the movement's great hallmarks. It is difficult to overstate the public influence evangelicalism has exerted through organizations like World Vision, Young Life, *Christianity Today*, or International Justice Mission. Or what about interdenominational schools like Westmont College or Gordon-Conwell Seminary? Would these collaborations

be possible without a theology that says personal faith in God matters more than allegiance to a church tradition? Where would these organizations be if not for voluntary contributions from individual evangelicals adhering to streamlined understandings of what makes for true faith? Rather than restricting God's work to the official channels of a church system, evangelical ecclesiology creates inherent possibilities for people to invest themselves on the basis of God's direct, personal prompting.

5. Impetus for action: Evangelicalism places a strong emphasis on passionate personal devotion to Jesus as a mark of Christian maturity. This facilitates a degree of vibrancy since active discipleship is expected and required of every person. Evangelicals understand that in order to reach as many people as possible with gospel, it's not enough for pastors to preach good sermons. Everyone has a role to play in learning to share their faith. More than any other stream of Christianity (Orthodox, Catholic, mainline Protestant), evangelicals value a certain degree of independence from the clergy. Such an ecclesiology is not only conducive to practical application and voluntary missional engagement, it champions high levels of lay participation. Not surprisingly, evangelicals have rightly come to emphasize biblical support for concepts like "the priesthood of all believers" and "the neighborhood as a mission field."

THE CONS

Spoiler alert: I conclude that evangelicalism is a mixed bag. It can beautiful or broken, but it's often both. When the brokenness seems all-consuming, we need reminders of the beauty. But when we're busy defending ourselves against the critics, we can gloss over what we've done wrong in the past—and continue doing wrong today. The solution isn't to dismantle the entirety of evangelicalism on account of its brokenness. Nor should we paint a rosy picture that minimizes systemic problems that have been pointed out for years. With the caveat that evangelicalism's structural deficiencies can be categorized in various ways, here are the top four that have led to the most damage in my view, particularly in the United States.

1. Celebrity dependence: Christendom's decline has placed evangelical churches into competition with one another for members. In order to maintain a following, celebrity pastors have arisen who not only draw a crowd but also function as authorities on matters of Scripture interpretation, political stances, and other public matters. The effect has been an increased reliance on fewer and fewer magnetic individuals (predominantly white men) to lead larger and larger groups of Christians, often in ways that clash with the stances of other celebrity pastors. The effect can be seen in the degree to which influential megachurch pastors shape public discourse through their provocative words and actions. The lack of structural accountability and connection with other churches hinders evangelical ecclesiology from moving beyond individualism's limits. Besides the free market and an internal governing board, who holds independent churches accountable? Tish Harrison Warren summarizes the effect:

> When Christian leaders become a brand, there are systems that would exalt and protect their brand over all else. There are systems that seek to maximize power

without the limits of institutional accountability. There are systems that seek to maximize profit without regard for the long-term flourishing and faithfulness of the broader church. Systemically, consumerism infects the church—both on the right and on the left.[5]

2. Thin ecclesiology: It's difficult to overstate the effect of individualism on American evangelicalism, which tends to truncate itself from continuity with tradition. When we foster the assumption that a relationship with Jesus is something exclusively personal, unmediated by a priest or community of faith, the result is decreased ecclesial awareness, of both the church universal and historic. As the body of Christ's well-being gives way to individuals' wide-ranging quests for fulfillment, the focus shifts inward toward a vague, church-less spirituality. Without consensus on what the church is or should be, smaller and smaller groups of Christians are left to determine the answers to increasingly bigger questions. George Hunsberger writes, "Resistance to religious intermediaries of any sort and belief in direct approach to God through Scripture, under the personal guidance of the Holy Spirit, contribute to an evangelical bias that sees Christian identity fundamentally as individual."[6]

3. Propensity for schism: As the church's intermediary role in spiritual life declines, American evangelicals have less incentive to join or remain active in a local fellowship of believers. Since church attendance is not strictly necessary for salvation, it becomes an optional realm competing with other extracurricular activities for Christians' involvement. When the church can't provide sufficiently engaging or

meaningful experiences, parishioners depart for greener pastures, not unlike customers who have shifted shopping habits. On a systems level, theological disputes prompt congregations to depart from their denominational families, sometimes to join another network but often to become independent. This results in less accountability, greater homogeneity, reduced theological dialogue, more new networks of churches in smaller clusters, and an overall increase in Christians' willingness to jump ship when their church community isn't an exact fit. You can't spell Protestant without protest!

4. Capitulation to idolatry and injustice: A strong case can be made that this is evangelicalism's greatest crisis today. If being ecclesiologically flimsy, doctrinally combative, and celebrity-driven were not enough, evangelicalism also has a proclivity to take its cues from prevailing ideologies and harmful narratives that hold America captive.[7] Whether it's Christian nationalism, consumerism, systemic racism, conspiracy theories, political polarization, toxic masculinity, xenophobia, or the doctrine of discovery, evangelicals in their worst moments have leveraged their influence to enable vices like these instead of resisting them in Jesus' name. Quick to speak and slow to listen, they have too often conformed to the patterns of this world in order to score victories in the culture wars, revealing insecurity about any phenomenon that could threaten their status in society. Like the previous three in this list, a lack of structural accountability makes it difficult to determine the church's posture beyond what is currently in vogue. When people tell me they're done with evangelicalism, its

complicity with injustice and capitulation to idolatry are the biggest reasons why.

When my college roommate interviewed for medical school, the interviewer asked why he chose Wheaton for his undergraduate studies. His response: "Because I wanted to receive the best Christian education I could." To which the interviewer replied, "Then what about Notre Dame?" At this point, my roommate realized he had used the word *Christian* as a synonym for *evangelical*, as many American evangelicals do. Evangelicals tend not to think of Notre Dame University as a *Christian* school because we actually mean *evangelical* when we say *Christian*. The prevalence of evangelical Christianity in the United States allows us to get away with imprecision.

Imprecise language has problems. Non-evangelical Christians don't know what we mean when we say "Christian," or perhaps they actually do and it's not the right meaning! Poor awareness of our own positionality leads to an inaccurate self-understanding. We confuse the broader category of Christianity with the narrow subset of evangelicalism. By conflating evangelicalism with Christianity, we who are evangelicals end up centering ourselves (whether consciously or not), which marginalizes others. We claim a monopoly that is not ours to claim. We put ourselves in God's place, judging others to be non-Christian if they don't look enough like us.

EVANGELICALISM SHAPING ME

Evangelicalism is my faith stream, the channel through which my spiritual, intellectual, vocational, and public life with God came alive in Jesus. Every story and experience described in this book wouldn't happen without evangelicalism shaping me. I've also been influenced by many non-evangelical Christians. But tracing back, it was in evangelical spaces where I first learned of their names and their work. As an undergraduate at Wheaton College, I learned that Jim Wallis and Tony Campolo were evangelicals too. I heard Brenda Salter McNeil speak in chapel. Their books introduced me to non-evangelicals like Oscar Romero, James Cone, Kosuke Koyama, and Wendell Berry. I was encouraged to learn from them.

In the eight years between college and seminary, I saw how the Religious Right claimed to speak for evangelicalism. The 2004 presidential election between George W. Bush and John Kerry was supposed to be the last time they influenced an election. But I can't count how many times I've heard the Religious Right pronounced dead or obsolete by the Religious Left.

I became a social worker because evangelicals taught me to integrate faith, work, and calling. Matthew 25 was huge for my understanding of discipleship. Alleviating and preventing poverty was an unquestionable calling, as I learned from my parents who were medical missionaries. During this time, I began wrestling with mixed feelings about the church. It drove me nuts sometimes, but I loved what it could become. Its actions regularly embarrassed me, but I knew I was complicit too.

I couldn't stop thinking about the church—theologically, structurally, historically, organizationally. I spent my spare time reading pastor blogs and ecclesiology books and visiting different denominations whenever I had the chance. One time I even visited seven churches in nine days, and I blogged about the strengths and weaknesses of each.[8]

As the conflict between the emerging church and the "young, restless, Reformed" movements heated up, I had my opinions too. It is in the past now, but I learned a lot from blogging about the questions raised. During this time I was influenced by Scot McKnight and David Gushee, and I started reading and following The Center for Public Justice and *Comment Magazine* online in my quest for a "third way" politically that valued the church's role.

Then as now, there were plenty of intra-evangelical spats to reflect on. Whether it was Rob Bell's book *Love Wins*, civil unions, the Manhattan Declaration, or support for the use of torture, I learned that evangelicals don't all agree. Noticing patterns of who usually aligned with who, I saw how the online chatter (not to mention my personal experience) wasn't universal to all Christians but unique to evangelical believers. Somewhere along the way, I stopped saying "Christianity" when I really meant evangelicalism.

From there, I noticed how evangelicalism in Hawai'i was stereotypically evangelical at times but also defied the brand. This was especially true when it came to denominations, demographics, and the ecclesial effect of geographic distance from the US mainland.[9] Throughout all this, what mattered to me was less how to vote or which theological system was correct. I cared most about what it means to be the church, warts and all. What do our collective patterns of sin tell us, especially when we don't seem to learn from our mistakes?

By the time I started my Master of Divinity at Fuller Seminary in 2011, I knew there were many ways to be an evangelical church. Denominational differences are no small thing, especially for women and minorities. The flavor matters. The demographics matter. And the geography; always the geography. This doesn't even get into my upbringing that included a formative decade outside the United States from age eight to eighteen. Evangelicalism was there, too, influencing how I relate to God, approach the Bible, and understand discipleship.

At the end of the day, it boils down to how we do life with God. For me, life with God is more than a Sunday thing, an afterlife thing, a prayer thing, a belief thing, a political thing, or a moral thing. Discipleship includes all those and more. At least that's what evangelicalism taught me.

PRACTICAL STEPS

In order to cultivate faith stream awareness among evangelicals, it would help tremendously if we became conversant with the particular aspects that distinguish our faith stream. Part of this means using precise language and de-centering ourselves from Christianity as a whole. From there, it's much easier to observe specific strengths and weaknesses. For example, if you're from a Baptist stream, you might appreciate the emphasis on evangelism or congregational polity, which translates to freedom from structural constraint at the local level. While Baptists sometimes make headlines for their conservative political stances, there's something to appreciate about how effective they have been in church planting and helping ordinary people experience transformation through a relationship with God. Baptists are often people of action, willing to take risks for the common good. It's difficult to mistake Albert Mohler for Martin Luther King Jr., but they are both Baptists, reminding us that the Southern Baptist Convention doesn't have a monopoly on this faith stream. Two of the most gifted preachers I've ever heard, Tony Campolo and Ken Fong, are both American Baptists (ABCUSA). Their messages are always practical, compelling, and focused on Jesus as they speak to the heart.

The question then is, How do we become aware of which stream we belong to? And once we find out, how does that awareness help us? Does it really matter which denomination we're part of as long as it's following Jesus? My answer is emphatically yes. It absolutely does matter. It matters for the same reason geography matters: to know your location. It matters for the same reason theology matters: to know if women can be pastors, or if Catholics are going to hell, or if this earth will be scorched to smithereens before the end comes. It matters for the same reason that ancestry matters: to know where you came from, what's in your DNA, and whose family you belong to. It matters for the same reason that ethnicity matters: to cherish the richness of one's heritage so that it's not whitewashed into a homogenizing agenda.

If geography, theology, ancestry, and ethnicity all matter, then yes, your faith stream matters too. Whether you realize it or not, these aspects have shaped you in profound ways.

Don't underestimate the power of awareness. With God's help, it can be the difference between harming and helping, confusion and insight, denial and honesty, despair and hope.

Part II

APPRECIATION

4

WHY APPRECIATION MATTERS

WHEN MY FAMILY LIVED IN ZAÏRE (now known as the Democratic Republic of the Congo), we regularly attended Bikuku Church, a local congregation worshiping in the Tshiluba language. A typical Sunday service lasted three hours or more. As a nine-year-old kid, I remember thinking the sermons would never end. My limited Tshiluba skills meant that I didn't understand most of what was spoken, but I learned a lot about Bikuku Church from what was communicated nonverbally. I observed that most people arrived on footpaths, wearing their Sunday best. Very few arrived by car—not even Americans like us, who walked along a path too narrow for vehicles wider than a motorcycle. There was no parking lot.

During the service itself, I remember being fascinated by the worship songs and dancing, as a sonic fusion of harmonies, clapping hands, and shuffling feet reverberated between cement walls and a sheet metal roof. One popular song used a call-and-response lyric of *démarrez*, French for "start your engines." When the song leader declared, "Démarrez!" the congregation would reply, "Vroom, vroom . . . vroom," accompanied by the hand motion of revving a motorcycle's throttle. As my mom explained to me, the song was about kickstarting your spiritual life with God, like an accelerating motorcycle.

Instead of passing an offering plate, congregants danced up and down the aisles as they left their gifts at the front. As I recall, the offering was the most celebratory part of the service. Sometimes there would even be additional offerings collected at multiple points in the worship gathering, with the vibe of an unplanned altar call in response to the Holy Spirit moving. If one were to describe a church in North America doing this, it might evoke images of the health and wealth movement, where monetary giving is encouraged to elicit a financial blessing from God. Although Bikuku Church would be considered financially poor by Western standards, I don't think the offerings were an attempt to gain wealth. One of my Congolese friends explained to me that the offering and dance are ways of praising God for bringing them through another week. The gift of being alive is worth celebrating, so the offering and dance are gifts to the God who gives life. I don't know how many of DR Congo's thirty million evangelicals[1] give their tithes and offerings in this manner, but I've never been to a church in the United States whose apex of the service was the offering!

Bikuku Church had no air conditioning, no video projector, no coffee bar, and no English spoken. And yet this, too, was evangelicalism. Here was a Presbyterian church but not the North American kind. Evangelical churches across the globe worship the living God in many different styles, but every church does so believing that Jesus makes a difference in people's lives. We come alive because Jesus is alive. He is the resurrection and the life we celebrate each week.

APPRECIATION BEFORE REPENTANCE?

Having looked at the importance of awareness, we come to the second posture: appreciation. Why does appreciation precede repentance? Shouldn't we begin with our brokenness before we get to the positive part? That would seem like the evangelical thing to do! In evangelical culture, it's common practice to begin presentations of the gospel with an acknowledgment of one's sinfulness and need for repentance. We're familiar with narratives that begin in darkness before reaching the light.

In Scripture, remembering often precedes renewal. Before the Israelites could enter the Promised Land, Moses pleaded with God's people to "remember how the LORD your God led you all the way in the wilderness these forty years" (Deuteronomy 8:2). Remembrance set the tone for their continued thriving with each other and with God.

Roughly six hundred years later, the people of God had forgotten their past lessons. Renewal in King Josiah's day began after a scroll of Scripture was found during the temple's renovation (2 Kings 22:8). This scroll, probably some form of Deuteronomy, was then read and followed, putting Israel back in touch with its Yahweh-centered institutional memory after years of worshiping other gods. Remembrance—and subsequent repentance—catalyzed reforms and renewal. Remembrance came first.

Fast forward to what Jesus tells the church at Sardis in the book of Revelation: "You have a reputation of being alive, but you are dead," Jesus declares. "Wake up! Strengthen what remains and is about to die." In case the church wonders how to do that, Jesus goes on to explain, "*Remember,* therefore, what you have received and heard; hold it fast, and *repent*" (Revelation 3:1-3, italics mine). Remembrance comes first.

Given all that is wrong with evangelicalism today, it's tempting to skip over appreciation and go straight to repentance. After all, there's a lot from which to repent! Even so, perhaps we can slow down to first *remember* and in remembering *appreciate.* Naming the good can highlight where the good ended too soon, got compromised, or didn't go far enough. When our remembrance leads us to repentance, we say yes to the possibility of better days ahead and to God's continued good work in this faith stream.

FAMILY TRAITS

Before you can solve your family's problems, it's worth acknowledging that you wouldn't be here if not for them. Appreciating your family does not mean tolerating abuse or endorsing everything they've done to you. It doesn't even mean that we like how things are going currently. My family of origin tends to be conflict avoidant and passive aggressive at times. We don't always do a good job expressing love directly through words or physical touch. After experiencing my wife's radically different family system, I could see how my family of origin could use improvement in these areas. Having said this, every family has strengths. It's unproductive to focus so much on our shortcomings that we forget the gift of being a family. My family has its share of negative patterns and tendencies, but it's still worth acknowledging and giving thanks for what they've given me.

After Rebecca and I had been married for a year, we moved back to my childhood home in Hawai'i to be caregivers for my dad. We transitioned from our cozy newlywed apartment in Chicagoland to sharing space with my family as I assisted with my dad's activities of daily living. Rebecca was surprised to see how Stringer mealtimes were so different from those in her Holmes family of origin. Holmes family dinners are warm and multi-layered as conversations overlap and sharing flows freely. By contrast, Stringer dinners are measured, allowing more space for listening, with one voice speaking at a time. Holmes dinners are like multi-voice choruses; everyone can chime in and sing harmony if they know how to do so, though slower speakers like myself struggle a bit to jump in the flow. Stringer dinners are like stunning arias—solos that can be appreciated on their own but can also keep others waiting for permission for their turn to sing. I appreciate that my family is very service oriented and knows how to offer and receive help. I also like that we are good listeners, more skilled at waiting our turn to speak than some other families I know. (Catch the passive-aggressiveness there?)

When it comes to evangelicalism, the same is true. Will we spend all our time discussing problems, or will we also do the work of remembering and appreciating that we even have a Christian family in the first place? We are far from a perfect family, yet at the same time there are discernible characteristics given to us by God and inherited from our evangelical ancestors that are worth naming. It can be easy to forget how evangelicalism got here and what it has given us. If there was no evangelicalism, perhaps we would not have been invited to follow Jesus or have a reason to engage the question of how to cultivate a healthier, less toxic evangelicalism.

APPRECIATING DENOMINATIONS

Time to tip my hand a bit on denominations. Over the course of my life, I've belonged to congregations in nine different Protestant denominations. You read that correctly. There were also a few nondenominational churches mixed in. Remember, we moved a lot. Some of these would be classified broadly as mainline Protestant, but each local church was shaped by evangelicalism in significant ways.

As mentioned in chapter one, my earliest years in Hawai'i were in a house church belonging to the United Church of Christ (UCC), part of the Congregationalist stream. Though my parents joined the Presbyterian Church (USA) as medical missionaries, we kept the UCC church as our home church. While overseas, we attended Bikuku Church in Zaïre (Presbyterian) and the International Protestant Church in Nepal (nondenominational). During my high school years as a dorm student in the Philippines, I went to Faith Fellowship (nondenominational). When our family returned home to Hawai'i, our UCC church had switched to the Evangelical Free Church (EFCA). During my first two years of college, I attended an Assemblies of God church. Then I joined Rebecca, who was working for a Filipino immigrant church in Chicago (EFCA), where we eventually got married. After returning to Hawai'i a year later, we briefly attended an Evangelical Covenant Church (ECC) before I was hired on staff at a Christian and Missionary Alliance (C&MA) church. Six years later, life circumstances led us to a church belonging to the Missionary Church USA but only briefly until Rebecca was hired by a Lutheran church (ELCA). That lasted until our second C&MA church hired us both on staff, where we stayed until moving to California to attend seminary. Once there, our family attended two different churches. Rebecca worked at a Presbyterian church (which switched from PCUSA to ECO during her time there) while I pursued ordination and attended our second ECC church. We've since moved back again to Hawai'i and now serve at the first ECC (Evangelical Covenant Church) we attended a number of churches ago. You can't make this stuff up!

Within this meandering faith stream of evangelicalism, I now belong to and am ordained in the Evangelical Covenant Church, a denomination whose six core affirmations shape my theology and approach to ministry:

1. The centrality of the Word of God

2. The necessity of the new birth

3. A commitment to the whole mission of the church

4. The church as a fellowship of believers

5. A conscious dependence on the Holy Spirit

6. The reality of freedom in Christ[2]

I love all the affirmations, but I especially appreciate *freedom in Christ*, which captures the idea that we avoid turning non-essentials into essentials. Perhaps you've already noticed this theme from my writing. For Covenanters, belief in Jesus is essential, whereas other matters of doctrine regarding baptism, the end times, and spiritual gifts are not.

REMEMBERING GOD'S ACTIONS

The act of remembering requires a degree of appreciation for what God has done and what his people have received. Like the children of Israel, we can be tempted to think that we've only received what we ourselves have produced. We forget that God gives us this ability in the first place: "You may say to yourself,

'My power and the strength of my hands have produced this wealth for me.' But remember the LORD your God, for it is he who gives you the ability to produce wealth, and so confirms his covenant, which he swore to your ancestors, as it is today" (Deuteronomy 8:17-18).

We may be tempted to think that evangelicalism is a solely human endeavor, rising and falling on its own merits. By removing God's action from the picture, we forget that our faith stream is not self-made but is received from those who go before us. Our evangelical ancestors, for better or worse, have passed down a particular form of Christianity that we've inherited as evangelicals. Spiritually speaking, we've eaten and been satisfied by the experience of encountering God in evangelical spaces. We've built fine houses of worship and settled into the comfort zone of our own evangelical sensibilities. Our herds and flocks confer status through expanded ministry platforms and name recognition. Now that evangelicalism is a global movement, will our hearts become proud? Will we forget the Lord's mighty hand and outstretched arm? When we appreciate God's gifts, passed down to us from spiritual ancestors who encountered Jesus through Scripture and prayer, the good work of remembering begins.

INDIVIDUAL AND COLLECTIVE STRENGTHS

Can evangelicalism's strengths help us address our weaknesses? To discern if the two are linked, let's test this theory on an individual. Let's say that one of my strengths is thoughtfulness and one of my weaknesses is perfectionism (hypothetically, of course). What is the relationship between thoughtfulness and perfectionism? At my best, I'm considerate and attentive to others; I consider the effect of my choices before making decisions; I don't act rashly or make big decisions lightly. This is all good. Yet at my worst, I'm prone to perfectionism, which hinders me from attempting tasks that might not succeed. My perfectionism can lead me to be overly critical of myself, hold myself to unrealistically high standards, and avoid taking risks that could be beneficial. I can be slow to begin important tasks because I don't want to fail or invite criticism. Such is the quandary of a thoughtful perfectionist.

Are thoughtfulness and perfectionism two sides of the same coin? The ingredients of thoughtfulness and perfectionism are similar. Both traits require the ability to think deeply and consider multiple perspectives. Both require a commitment to quality, accuracy, and effectiveness. The question then becomes, Does appreciating my thoughtfulness help me address my perfectionism? If so, the benefit of appreciation is more than just confidence or a positive self-image. There's also a way in which the good helps counteract the bad. Instead of beating myself up for my perfectionism, I can face it with less fear because I know that perfectionism is really just thoughtfulness gone awry. In other words, I can resist perfectionism by embracing thoughtfulness. Without appreciating what's good, I can't properly address what's bad.

Furthermore, focusing on negative traits makes it easier to become cynical and lose hope. If all I am is a perfectionist dominated by perfectionism, I will fail to give my thoughtfulness its proper due. Counteracting what's bad involves cultivating what's good. Stopping deforestation isn't enough; we must also plant trees. It's important to lament what's wrong with evangelicalism while also acknowledging and affirming its strong points. Both are vital.

If a personal strength like thoughtfulness can be traced to the same ingredients as a weakness like perfectionism, such a link further underscores why appreciation matters to evangelicalism's health as a space. This is why good coaches affirm what athletes do well. Good parents affirm positive behaviors seen in their kids. Good teachers affirm what they see their students doing right. Good doctors affirm healthy habits in their patients. When I see my kids misbehave, it's not enough to say, "Don't do that." I must also look for opportunities to praise them for doing the right thing.

During my time in social work, I was taught the *strengths perspective*.[3] One way to understand what social workers do is to realize that they are the ones sent in to clean up the messes made in society: homelessness, drug addiction, child abuse, mental illness, poverty. Anyone who wants to address these problems will cross paths with a social worker sooner or later. Like custodians sent to the parts of a building where a mess has been made (regardless of who made it), social workers go to the places in society that need cleaning up. It would be easy for social workers to have a problem-based approach. Find the problem; fix the problem. It sounds counterproductive to talk about what's going well when there's a problem that needs attention.

That's where the strengths perspective comes in. Instead of focusing on a client's weaknesses and deficiencies (housing, sobriety, safety, health, money), we choose to focus on a client's strengths and resources. A veteran might be homeless, but he does have a steady income. A child is at risk for abuse, but she has strong self-advocacy skills. A patient cannot work full-time, but she belongs to a supportive network of family and friends.

STRENGTHS-BASED EVANGELICALISM

I propose that we adopt a strengths-based perspective on evangelicalism, at least some of the time. If you're a blue-state city-dweller like me and your politics lean left, my guess is that you probably have an awareness of what evangelical Christianity has done wrong. You might roll your eyes at the mention of Franklin Graham or Jerry Falwell Jr. You've seen the need for repentance so much that perhaps it's all you can see. If this is you, let me tell you that appreciation matters for evangelicalism, especially if we're going to avoid the danger of cynicism. Like good social workers, let's not minimize evangelicalism's problems or its strengths. The more weaknesses we see, the more important it becomes to see strengths. This isn't license to be triumphalistic about how great we are, but there's a downside to denying the bright side. Remember the strengths perspective. You might be surprised by what you find.

Before looking at specific strengths of evangelicalism, I offer an important caveat: not everyone agrees on what those strengths are. Furthermore, we might disagree on whether an attribute of evangelicalism is even a strength or a weakness to begin with. For example, is it an asset or a liability that evangelicals emphasize a personal relationship with God? As soon as one person names a strength, another person will point out the shadow side of that trait, not unlike thoughtfulness and perfectionism. Once we start naming positive aspects, it's not long before counterexamples emerge showing how those blessings have been twisted into curses.

Imagine a classroom teacher asking a room full of evangelicals to raise their hands before answering the question, "What is one of evangelicalism's strengths?" The first person raises her hand and says, "Well, I think it's a strength that evangelicals love to study the Bible and take seriously how it applies to their lives." Another hand pops up with the counter argument: "Yes, but evangelicals have been so heavy-handed with the Bible that they've used it as a weapon to exclude and oppress others."

The teacher re-asks the question, "What is another one of evangelicalism's strengths?" A different person raises his hand and says, "Evangelicals have a strong desire to know Jesus personally and live as his disciples." No sooner are the words out of his mouth than the counterargument comes from the back row: "Yes, but American evangelicals have a hyperindividualistic and whitewashed understanding of Jesus that glosses over his rough edges and neglects the parts of his teaching that got him killed by the religious establishment."

The teacher re-asks the question a third time, "What is another strength of evangelicalism?" A brave soul puts forward a reply: "Evangelicalism values the active participation of laypeople. We don't just spectate while the priest does everything for us." And again, the counterargument isn't far behind: "It's true that laypeople do a lot of good ministry, but we're also the ones who seem more beholden to watching celebrity pastors preach than any other stream of Christianity. In our efforts to reach the masses, we've turned church into a spectator sport."

On and on the discussion goes. With every strength comes a corresponding weakness. Back and forth, like thoughtfulness versus perfectionism. How can we escape this cycle? Is there no way to converse about evangelicalism's strengths without turning it into another discussion about weaknesses? How are we supposed to untangle evangelicalism's merits from its defects?

TAKING JESUS SERIOUSLY

Even if we don't agree on which of evangelicalism's aspects we should appreciate, hopefully we can acknowledge the existence of good aspects. The question then becomes, What should we do with the good parts? I believe the answer starts with appreciating them.

For example, I appreciate that evangelicalism takes Jesus seriously. We spend a lot of time discussing the significance of Jesus and the difference he makes in our lives. Even when we get it wrong, it's usually because we've misunderstood what it means to take Jesus seriously, not because we don't care about Jesus.

When my parents signed on as missionaries with the Presbyterian Church, they didn't go to Zaïre as pastors or evangelists. They went as medical missionaries because of their evangelical faith expressing itself in action. Their daily work focused more on earthly life than the afterlife, but they didn't see themselves as second class missionaries. Some thirty years later, I became curious about what still exists of IMCK (Christian Medical Institute of the Kasai region), the mission my parents belonged to in Zaïre. I discovered that it's still there, continuing the work through the same hospital (Bon Berger/Good Shepherd) at Tshikaji where my youngest sister, Amy, was born. The dental clinic my dad helped to start in 1988 is still there, too, and his name even got mentioned in an IMCK newsletter over ten years after his passing and twenty-five years since he was last in the country. A wave of gratitude came over me as I scrolled through photos of familiar people and places I hadn't seen since age ten. These priceless memories are the byproduct of my parents taking Jesus seriously. Their work in providing quality medical care and education continues.

Someone in our thought experiment could rightly ask, "What about colonialism? How do you reconcile your parents work in the Congo with the historic patterns of inequity perpetuated there, including by American missionaries?" A fair question. Truth is, I'm still processing my own relationship with colonialism. Similar to inhabiting an evangelical space, there's no point in denying my embeddedness within an unjust setup that benefits people like me. In the West, we perpetuate the illusion of distance from colonialism by acting like it can be adopted or rejected, with the goal of not touching the hot potato. In reality, it's already baked into our history. The question isn't how to avoid getting burned but how to stop the fire.

My time in Zaïre taught me that Christianity is not inherently Western. It doesn't have to be. Each place takes Jesus seriously in their own way, no matter how much they might insist that their way is the right way. What makes evangelicalism distinct, then, is not its location or culture-specific expressions—because those vary significantly. Its distinguishing features are the parts that remain consistent across continents: the centrality of Jesus and the call to make disciples, expressed throughout the week, not just on Sundays—or on Saturdays, like the church in Nepal where my family lived after Zaïre. Appreciation matters because without it we confuse the packaging with the gifts. There will always be packaging. We can't get rid of that, but we can appreciate the distinctions between the universal and contextual aspects of our faith.

Appreciation results in a capacity to see both strengths and weaknesses, good and bad, all taken together as part of the whole.

True appreciation sees things clearly, without denial or white-washing. To say that evangelicalism is all good or all bad is a false dichotomy. Martin Luther's framework of *simul iustus et peccator,* simultaneously saint and sinner, points in that direction. The more that evangelicals grasp this dynamic, the clearer we'll see evangelicalism's complex realities. We are all saints and sinners—both as individuals and collectively as the church.

5

STRENGTHENING OUR STRENGTHS

MY FRIEND MARK GREW UP attending a Pentecostal church in New Jersey's Ocean County. His family was at the church building not only each Sunday but also Monday (for worship practice), Thursday (for youth worship practice), and Friday (for youth service). The congregation of about 750 was predominately white and held conservative political views. Mark remembers there being a strong focus on revivalism and its outward expressions. People who could outwardly show how they were being touched by the Spirit—via tears, laughter, tongues, being slain in the Spirit (they called it "falling out")—were thought to be more in tune with God. This often led to people pursuing those types of manifestations of the Holy Spirit for their own sake. People who did not express themselves in this way were thought to be spiritually deficient. The church was committed to culture war issues such as abortion, the "homosexual agenda" (a catch-all term used for anything related to LGBTQ+ concerns), and family values, and had little patience for people, even other Christians, with different viewpoints. The church viewed mainline churches with pity at best, thinking they didn't believe in the fullness of the Christian life, or with suspicion, thinking they only preached a "social gospel," which wasn't real. It also viewed the Catholic Church as outside the true Christian faith.

Despite all this, Mark's church wasn't all bad. There were positive aspects too. Mark remembers the time three adults prayed for him at a youth group event. These adults took turns praying for every kid there and had seemingly important words of prophecy for many of them. There were a lot of tears from adults and teens alike. Mark was the last one—a pretty quiet, reserved, mild-tempered thirteen-year-old. When it was finally Mark's turn to receive prayer, the adults spontaneously and immediately started laughing hysterically—for a long time. Mark describes this time period as being "long enough for my self-conscious teenage self to be convinced I had something hanging out of my nose or something." Finally, they explained that they perceived that God delighted in Mark as a person. They affirmed that Mark was an encourager and was meant to be an encouragement to others and should actively cultivate that gift. "I have had some bad experiences with prophetic words as well, over the years," Mark recalls, "but all these years later I spend a lot of my day doing my best to encourage people." For Mark, who grew up to be a clinical social worker, this moment as a thirteen-year-old was an example of being seen and known by the God who made him. Those memorable words of affirmation were possible because three adults were willing to tune their ears to listen for God's voice—a very evangelical thing to do.

Here's what Mark said when I asked what he appreciates most about growing up in that church:

The people genuinely cared for one another. It did often feel like a family. There were adults who I felt actually cared about me. One of them even took me to buy my first electric guitar. The other day I found a note dated 1995 from an older woman in the church that simply said "God likes you exactly as you are." It must have meant something to me as a teenager, because I kept it. I think the relationships were authentic and people generally wanted to be there for each other. There was a recognition that people have different strengths or gifts and we do well to honor and cultivate those gifts. This approach helped prepare me for the "strengths-based" language of social work. There was real effort to instill a faith that was holistic, that touched every part of a person's life. And there was the belief that our relationship with God is reflected in our relationship with others, especially vulnerable people. As practical applications of this belief, we had things like "nursing home ministry" and "prison ministry."[1]

Despite the fact that this particular expression of evangelicalism struggled with nationalism, hyperspiritualism, anti-intellectualism, and was, in Mark's words, "a little obsessed with hell and holiness," it still had an observable faithfulness and commitment to Christian living based on Philippians 2:12, a call to "work out your salvation." For all its faults, this church offered a real sense of belonging, which Mark says helped instill in him the value of Christian community, a desire to see his faith affect all aspects of his daily life, and an appreciation for mystery and mysticism. The evangelicalism of Mark's youth wasn't all good, but it wasn't all bad either.

Through his steady refusal to see only one side of it, I see Mark as someone who has helped me cultivate appreciation for evangelicalism. Even though he no longer attends this type of church, he hasn't given up on Pentecostal expressions of Christianity. In fact, he now appreciates more than before its roots in racial justice, original commitment to nonviolence/pacifism, and what Mark playfully calls its "overall strangeness."

WHEN APPRECIATION IS HARD

Of the four postures proposed in this book, appreciation might be the most difficult to cultivate, especially if you carry significant baggage from negative experiences in church. It might seem arrogant or naive to highlight evangelicalism's positive traits, especially when its negative traits factor prominently in your mind. If the church has inflicted harm on you or your loved ones, it's fair to ask first if it's even appropriate to cultivate appreciation for the place that caused such damage. This book's purpose isn't to foster a kind of Stockholm syndrome whereby you're taught to sympathize with an abuser. I don't want to drum up positive regard for an entity that hasn't made any positive impact in your life.

If evangelicalism has done nothing but cause pain and confusion in your life, I don't want to excuse this in any way by promoting a search for something that isn't there. This book is primarily for readers who have *mixed* feelings about evangelicalism. Your emotions toward evangelicalism are more likely to be mixed if your experience hasn't been all bad or all good. Therefore, my purpose in this chapter is to focus on the part that hasn't been all bad. If there's really nothing you can honestly appreciate about evangelicalism, then so be it. But if there's even a small segment of your evangelical experience that has been helpful or worthwhile, I believe it's worth unpacking what that is so that it, too, can be given its due. My guess is that if your experience with evangelicalism has been mixed, there are probably aspects that benefited you in some way. The question then becomes, Which aspects are they?

FOSTERING COLLECTIVE MEMORY

Evangelicals generally recognize the value of journaling on an individual level. To resist the clamor fueled by a heaping pile of seemingly urgent concerns, we pause to look back at what God has done for us. "I will remember the deeds of the LORD; / yes, I will remember your miracles of long ago. / I will consider all your works / and meditate on all your mighty deeds" (Psalm 77:11-12).

A few verses later, the psalmist recalls a specific event when God showed up at just the right time. God's people had just escaped from Pharaoh's oppressive rule but were now trapped by the Red Sea as Pharaoh's army closed in behind them. What followed became one of the Old Testament's most dramatic rescue stories. God parted the Red Sea, his people passed safely through the waters, then God closed the sea to drown their oppressors. It was a miracle that God's people would always remember. "Your path led through the sea, / your way through the mighty waters, / though your footprints were not seen" (Psalm 77:19).

A church that understands its history is better prepared to discern where it will be headed in the future. These stories remind us of who God is and who we are as God's beloved people.

That's why we recall stories from the past on both a personal *and* collective level. We can't appreciate what we don't remember. By remembering these things, our appreciation grows for how far God has brought us. Psalm 111:2-4 declares, "Great are the works of the LORD; / they are pondered by all who delight in them. / Glorious and majestic are his deeds, / and his righteousness endures forever. / He has caused his wonders to be remembered; / the LORD is gracious and compassionate."

Appreciation does not deny failure. We can appreciate how God used Moses without denying the effect of Moses' costly mistakes along the journey. We can appreciate how God's wandering people feasted on bread falling from heaven in the wilderness without denying the idolatry of the golden calf. We can appreciate how lives were transformed by the New Testament church without denying the unhealthy patterns that marked churches like the ones in Corinth and Laodicea.

In the Bible, we see God's people cultivating more than just personal memories of God's goodness expressed to individuals. The Psalms weren't written primarily with private devotional use in mind but were meant to be prayed and sung by God's people together. The Psalms compose the prayer book of God's gathered people, summoning us to remember where we've been on our journey with God, not just as individual believers but also as a community. At the Last Supper, Jesus instructed his disciples to remember him by eating bread and drinking wine together, a communal form of remembrance. "And he took bread, gave thanks and broke it, and gave it to them, saying, 'This is my body given for you; do this in remembrance of me'" (Luke 22:19).

"Since we are receiving a kingdom that cannot be shaken, let us be thankful, and so worship God acceptably with reverence and awe" (Hebrews 12:28). Notice how it says *let us* be thankful. This is collective memory.

To practice appreciation through collective memory, here are some questions to ask:

- What does this church do well?
- Where is God at work in this church's ministry?
- What does this church's fruit look like in people's lives?
- What does this church communicate about who God is?
- How does the church care for its community?

A LEGACY OF SEEKING JUSTICE

In a series of mass shootings at three spas in the Atlanta area on March 16, 2021, eight people were killed, including six women of Asian descent. On March 28, an estimated five thousand people gathered in fourteen cities across the United States as part of the National Rally for AAPI Lives and Dignity.[2] The event was organized by the Asian American Christian Collaborative, a group founded a year earlier in response to the rise of overt anti-Asian racism during the Covid-19 pandemic. Michelle Ami Reyes, AACC's vice president, described the rally's significance: "This effort is historic. There has never been a coordinated national effort like this by the greater Asian American Christian community to stand for AAPI lives and dignity and to show the country that we will not be silent against hate crimes hurting our community as well as other communities of color."[3]

A cursory survey of AACC's leadership team reveals a concentration of pastors with ties to prominent evangelical organizations: Wheaton College, Zondervan, InterVarsity, *Christianity*

Today, Fuller Seminary, and the Christian Community Development Association. The leaders of AACC aren't just Asian American Christians. They are evangelicals too. Theologian Sue-Jeanne Koh traces how Asian American Christian theology reflects a history of evangelical spaces overlooking Asian American church leaders who on one hand face pressure to conform as a "model minority" while being marginalized as "perpetual foreigners" on the other.[4] This is part of why AACC's work is necessary.

For a generation of Asian American Christians who did not grow up hearing stories of their ancestors taking a stand for justice, this kind of activism might seem like a recent development. It's not. Tim Tseng, a historian of Asian American Christianity, suggests that "progressive-minded evangelicals and non-evangelicals need to retrieve the stories of Asian and Asian American Christians in the early and mid-20th century. They may discover that many of these Christians articulated a social justice-oriented gospel—sometimes through a liberal theological framework—but more often, through an evangelical idiom."[5]

In an interview about his book *Brown Church*, historian Robert Chao Romero, the son of a Mexican father and a Chinese immigrant mother, points out that it isn't new for followers of Jesus to be justice-oriented. "Over the last 500 years, probably 85 percent of institutional Christianity has sided with colonialism and slavery ... and manifest destiny," he contends. "But there's always been that voice of 15 percent or so that has stood up in the name of Jesus against injustice."[6]

As we identify aspects of evangelicalism to appreciate, let's be careful to give credit where it's due. I'm not saying that evangelicalism's predominantly white institutions can take credit for the efforts made by people of color on the margins. I'm saying we can thank God for groups like AACC and movements like the Brown Church who enrich evangelical spaces by continuing the legacy of a holistic gospel that values both evangelism and social justice. This legacy is one of evangelicalism's undervalued treasures that merits greater appreciation. Through it, God provides sustenance and hope in a hostile wilderness. Our golden calves don't negate God's bread from heaven.

Here are some ways to cultivate appreciation for evangelicalism:

- *Cite your sources.* Notice, and give thanks for, features of evangelicalism that help people encounter and follow Jesus. When evangelicalism is the means through which someone acquired a certain skill, sensibility, or value, it's important to not only know where it came from but also to name where it came from. Schools call this citing your sources. For example, if an evangelical youth group or campus ministry taught you how to grapple with Scripture's meaning and to put into practice the implications of its claims, you can cultivate an appreciation for this not only by expressing what you appreciate but also by attributing it to evangelicalism.

- *Learn about Christian faith streams beyond evangelicalism.* The more I learn from my Roman Catholic friends, the more I appreciate evangelicalism. I have options. My evangelicalness becomes more of a choice and less of an obligation. Connecting dots between denominational and geographic diversity has been a significant area of learning for me. Perhaps I acted out my nomadic upbringing by searching for an ecclesial home that rooted my story in something bigger than me, all the while acknowledging the contingent relativity of this arrangement. Experiencing the effect of geographic change and cultural relativity taught me to look for ways in which ecclesial expressions are contingent upon certain factors.

- *Read and recommend books by evangelicals of color.* If we want to stop stereotyping evangelicalism as exclusively white, we need to value writers and leaders who teach from a different vantage point. When we read books by evangelicals of color, we're reminded that this is a diverse movement with much to offer. Take a look at your bookshelf, whether it contains paper books or ebooks. What percentage of the Christian books are written by white male authors? How many are written by women or men of color? If people of color comprise a third of evangelicals, shouldn't this be reflected in what we read? The first time I did this exercise, I saw my bookshelf in a new way.

Books by Evangelicals of Color

Bread for the Resistance, Donna Barber

Unsettling Truths, Mark Charles and Soong-Chan Rah

Mixed Blessing, Chandra Crane

Rethinking Incarceration, Dominique Gilliard

Is Christianity the White Man's Religion? Antipas Harris

Mother to Son, Jasmine Holmes

The Beautiful Community, Irwyn Ince

Raise Your Voice, Kathy Khang

Liberation Is Here, Nikole Lim

Reading While Black, Esau McCaulley

Roadmap to Reconciliation, Brenda Salter McNeil

The Minority Experience, Adrian Pei

Prophetic Lament, Soong-Chan Rah
Learning to Be, Juanita Campbell Rasmus
Brown Church, Robert Chao Romero
Healing Racial Trauma, Sheila Wise Rowe
Beyond Colorblind, Sarah Shin
Permission to Be Black, A. D. Thomason
The Color of Compromise, Jemar Tisby
Rescuing the Gospel from the Cowboys, Richard Twiss
The Next Worship, Sandra Maria Van Opstal

- *Spread faith stream awareness and foster collective memory.*
  The greater our faith stream awareness, the more we'll appreciate evangelicalism's positive traits. I didn't learn that
  I was an evangelical Christian until I had spent almost two
  decades in the church. How could I appreciate something I
  didn't know existed? In the decades since my first "Theology of Culture" class at Wheaton College, how has appreciation been cultivated in my life? Asking *how* this happened is a good question, but it can't be answered without
  also asking *who* helped me cultivate this appreciation, because it didn't happen in isolation. The process of gaining
  an appreciation for evangelicalism didn't happen all at
  once. It began with receiving basic knowledge of what it
  was, followed by an awareness of my connection to it. From
  there, I grappled with the positive and negative ways my
  connection to evangelicalism both benefited and hindered
  my own discipleship. If I had to list the key experiences that
  cultivated my appreciation for evangelicalism, I would say
  it was a mix of identifying the particularities of my own
  faith stream as well as experiencing a taste of other streams.

- *Build on your strengths*. If you wanted someone to appreciate Italian food, wouldn't it make sense to cook them some delicious Italian food? You would highlight ingredients like olive oil, oregano, garlic, and tomatoes. The better it tastes, the more they will appreciate the cuisine. Consider evangelicalism as a type of cuisine that has been prepared and served to millions of hungry souls over the past two hundred years. If you appreciate evangelicalism's passion for putting faith into action, you can cultivate this in others by letting them see your faith in action. If people affirm this quality in you and ask where you learned it, you can share the source. Yes, it was from Jesus, but you experienced Jesus through evangelicalism. If Jesus has worked in your life through multiple faith streams, it's worth affirming these details with greater precision.

PRACTICAL PEOPLE

I love the practicality of my evangelical people. I may not always agree with others' specific methods or conclusions, but I appreciate their sincere efforts to put faith into action. Just look at how many books evangelicals publish every year. Most of them are aimed at pursuing life change of some kind. There's a strong desire to make an impact and get things right. You can accuse evangelicals of being too simplistic, too intense, too rigid, or too literal, but the one thing you can't accuse us of is being too inaccessible or hard to understand. Evangelicals care about walking our talk. We care about where the rubber meets the road, whether our relationship with God is genuine or not. Yes, we might fall for politicians whose faith is just a façade to get more votes, but what you won't hear us say is that faith doesn't matter to us or that our votes have nothing to do with our values. We understand that votes and values are inextricably linked.

UNITY AND PARTICULARITY

Given the many divisions between evangelicals today, what is the path to unity? Should we smooth over our denominational and cultural differences in order to unite under the banner of evangelicalism? Not so fast. Unity is important and close to Jesus' heart, "that all of them may be one" (John 17:21), but our unity must also take seriously our particularity as every people and tongue (Revelation 7). We probably shouldn't preach about the unity in John 17 until we've grappled with the diversity in Revelation 7. If this book helps to foster unity around the common ground we share in Christ, I'm all for it. *Interdenominational collaboration* is part of evangelicalism's distinct character, whether we name it or not. That said, a healthy approach to unity will not come at the expense of evangelicals on the margins, who are yet again asked to accommodate the mainstream in order to fit in. This requires those with more power to adopt an expanded understanding of what evangelical spaces can look like. Evangelicalism is already diverse within the United States—not to mention globally. I believe that only when we acknowledge and affirm evangelicalism's diversity (not just ethnic and linguistic but also in worship style, politics, and theological ethos) can we pursue Christ-centered unity around areas of common ground: Jesus, Scripture, and an intimately direct experience of the divine.

Despite its diversity, evangelicalism often struggles to handle differences in belief, style, politics, and ethos. How do we distinguish between essentials and nonessentials? Without a pope or centralized system for making decisions, there can be many different criteria for assessing this. We can't disagree about whether Jesus is the Savior, but what about speaking in tongues or the age of the earth? At what point do we have sufficient grounds for breaking fellowship? Similar to the danger of coming together without bringing our particularity with us, we run the risk of a family split when we move too quickly. We cut people off and excommunicate them, thinking this is a good thing when it actually perpetuates the problem. When we settle for cheap unity, we can lose appreciation for evangelicalism's diversity.

The end goal for appreciation is less about improving evangelicalism's image before others and more about seeing the fullness of God's goodness as expressed through the diversity of his church. The goal of appreciation is giving gratitude and thanksgiving to God for the gift. When we minimize our own strengths and resources, we miss an opportunity to taste and savor the sweetness of the church at its best. Rob Bell once said about the church, "It is the most frustrating institution in the world. And yet, when it's firing on all cylinders, there's absolutely nothing like it."[7]

There's more to appreciation than reducing self-loathing. It's also about increasing a healthy love for our best selves. I don't believe that everyone who has experienced evangelicalism is in a position to appreciate it. But for those who are, appreciation points to a God who gives good gifts to his children. When we have eyes to appreciate what we've been generously given, I believe we become less afraid to admit what we've wrongfully taken from others. As we learn to better distinguish the church's strengths from its shortcomings, we reduce the risk of confusing hope with harm. A child who knows when to say, "Thank you, I appreciate you," is a child who can learn when to say, "I'm sorry, I was wrong."

Part III

REPENTANCE

6

EVIL CLOAKED IN SPIRITUAL LANGUAGE

ONE OF THE MOST INTENSELY MEANINGFUL sessions at the Urbana 18 student missions conference focused on repentance. Recounting how the church has historically perpetrated evil and been complicit with injustice, a video called *A Litany* listed examples of Christianity's most costly failures around the world. At one point, the narrator says:

> Martin Luther's writings made him an icon of the German church, but in his words were the seeds of anti-Semitism. His words paved the way for the Holocaust. In South Africa, the justification for Apartheid was written in a Christian seminary by Christian theologians. We cloaked evil in spiritual language. Our theology helped birth segregation, subjugation, and genocide.

The narrator continues, "When European settlers and missionaries landed in America, they were backed by the Doctrine of
Discovery, a church ruling that said Christians could subjugate
the indigenous peoples who already lived on this land. 'Enemies
of Christ' we called them, rather than beloved image-bearers of
God. Their bodies. Their ground. Over them we built our cities,
our homes. We did this. Can we see it?"[1]

We can't understand the harm endured by our indigenous and
Native siblings in Christ without accounting for the doctrine of
discovery. As we think about where to begin the dialogue, a metaphor from Mark Charles stays with me:

> It feels like our indigenous peoples are an old grandmother
> who lives in a very large house. It is a beautiful place with
> plenty of rooms and comfortable furniture. But years ago,
> some people came into her house and locked her upstairs
> in the bedroom. Today her home is full of people. They are
> sitting on her furniture. They are eating her food. They are
> having a party in her house. They have since come upstairs
> and unlocked the door to her bedroom, but now it is much
> later, and she is tired, old, weak, and sick; so she can't or
> doesn't want to come out. But what is the most hurtful and
> what causes her the most pain is that virtually no one from
> this party ever comes upstairs to find the grandmother in
> the bedroom. No one sits down next to her on the bed,
> takes her hand, and simply says, "Thank you. Thank you for
> letting us be in your house."[2]

WHAT IS REPENTANCE?

Why does repentance matter? That sounds like an easy one.
Scripture is packed with descriptions of repentance and

instructions stressing its importance. There is no sinner's prayer without admitting that you're a sinner. Repentance is foundational to discipleship. Jesus starts his ministry with a call to repentance. Following his temptation by the devil in the wilderness, Jesus begins preaching with the words, "Repent, for the kingdom of heaven has come near" (Matthew 4:17). Right out of the gate, Jesus draws a connection between repentance and the kingdom of heaven.

When the very first Christian church was launched in Jerusalem, the apostle Peter preached a sermon explaining the significance of Jesus' life, death, and resurrection. After hearing this message, the people were cut to the heart and asked Peter and the other apostles, "What shall we do?" Peter began his reply this way: "Repent and be baptized, every one of you, in the name of Jesus Christ for the forgiveness of your sins" (Acts 2:37-38). Attempting to follow Jesus without repentance is like trying to play solitaire without knowing what a deck of cards is. There's no discipleship without repentance. If repentance is so straightforward, why do we need a whole chapter on its importance for evangelicalism?

The answer depends on what is being asked. If we're talking about placing one's trust in Jesus, that would be one thing. It's easy to see the importance of repentance for personal salvation. But if we're asking why repentance matters to evangelicalism as a shared space, the question becomes one about collective repentance. Is it possible for evangelicalism to repent collectively? If we did, what would that even look like?

Individual sins certainly matter, but they aren't the only sins that matter. Individualism says, "The sins of others aren't my fault," but collective repentance is a longstanding biblical practice for God's people. Collective sins require collective repentance. Until we acknowledge how we have fractured shalom with God, neighbor, and creation, we cannot begin to make right what has gone wrong. Individuals pray a sinner's prayer, but the church prays a sinners' prayer. Catch the distinction? The apostrophe's location makes a huge difference.

FROM PERSONAL TO COMMUNAL REPENTANCE

Communal repentance matters because communities matter to God. In Scripture we find God speaking not just to one person at a time but to households, churches, cities, and entire ethnic groups. From a practical standpoint, it makes sense that Scripture texts were written with larger audiences in mind. If the text is written down, its message can be received by many individuals who either read it or hear it read to them. God addresses groups of people so that they all hear the same message.

Evangelicals care about this too. With the advent of mass media communication, the modern evangelical church broadcasted its message to thousands of people at a time, thanks to radio, television, taped recordings, and eventually the internet. Evangelicals are no strangers to God's Word being preached to large groups.

Growing an audience to expand your message's reach makes sense, but that's not the only reason God speaks the same message to more than one person at a time. It's not just that the prophets (who spoke for God) wanted to multiply their impact, save time, or build a following. The prophets spoke to communities because God cares about how communities live together.

It's not enough to focus on doing the right thing personally. It also matters that groups of people take the right actions together. Any decision made by a church elder board, state legislature, group of company shareholders, married couple, or parent-teacher association is a collective action.

In the words of Rich Villodas, "The Bible is more communal than individual. Jesus teaches us to pray 'Our Father' not 'My Father.' Paul uses the phrase, 'our Lord' 53 times, & 'my Lord' only 1 time. 'Jesus is my personal savior' is not found in Holy Scripture. We are the people of God. We belong to each other."[3]

As the Israelites make their journey toward the Promised Land, God addresses them as a plurality of hearers. "Hear, Israel, and be careful to obey so that it may go well with you and that you may increase greatly in a land flowing with milk and honey, just as the LORD, the God of your ancestors, promised you. Hear, O Israel: The LORD our God, the LORD is one" (Deuteronomy 6:3-4).

The vast majority of New Testament letters were written to a plural audience: local churches. The book of Revelation's original readers included seven different congregations in Asia Minor. Nehemiah is an example of an individual who repented corporately. "I confess the sins we Israelites, including myself and my father's family, have committed against you. We have acted very wickedly toward you. We have not obeyed the commands, decrees and laws you gave your servant Moses" (Nehemiah 1:6-7).

Collective sin and collective repentance are not foreign to the Bible. If anything, the American evangelical church's tendency to focus exclusively on personal sin and personal repentance is imposed onto Scripture. Think about what we focus on during the top three Christian festivals of Christmas, Easter, and Pentecost. Christmas celebrates the birth of my personal Lord and Savior. Easter celebrates Jesus dying for me so that I can gain my personal salvation. Pentecost, as the church's birthday, becomes

the anniversary of my personal religious club, the place that supplies me with my personal sense of belonging and purpose. I'm
exaggerating for effect, but the point is that the gospel isn't just
for individuals—it's also for groups.

Mark Noll writes about evangelicalism's proclivity for individual-
centered theology: "What evangelicalism has been great at doing
is bringing life back to cold religious form. But, evangelicalism is
a parasitic movement. The great evangelical leaders are not theo-
reticians of institutions. Some of them are very good theologians
on questions of personal salvation. They're not theologians of
culture, they're not theologians of society. There are problems with
the Christian outreach that is just the theology of society, but
there are also problems when the individual attention is so strong
that culture and society is lost sight of."[4]

Evangelicalism's focus on personal faith isn't wrong, just incomplete. Faith stream awareness (see chapter 3) constitutes an
essential ingredient of communal repentance. When our faith
can hum along merrily without collective awareness, it shows
that individualism has gone too far. This hyperindividualist
lens is precisely what we need to repent of first because until
we do that, we won't be able to see evangelicalism's collective
sins as problems that affect us. Just like a pre-repentant
Christian may not grasp the severity of their sin because they
see themselves as a good enough person without an urgent
need for a Savior, so, too, a person without faith stream
awareness might not be able to see evangelicalism's collective
sins and the need for collective repentance.

Here's the good news: once we develop faith stream awareness
of what evangelicalism is, our eyes can be opened to see not
only our collective sins but also the pathway toward collective

repentance and restoration. We need more than a sinner's prayer in the singular. Evangelicalism needs to learn sinners' prayers— plural confessions for plural people.

WALLS AND WEALTH GAPS

For a three-year period starting when was I was seven, my family lived in Kananga, Zaïre, for my dad's work as a missionary dentist. At that time, Kananga was known as the world's largest city without electricity, where half a million people managed without paved roads, telephones, or traffic signals. The entire city had two restaurants, one dry goods store, and a utility company that turned on the water supply for two hours each day. Most of our food came from peddlers who brought produce to our house, which my mother would carefully inspect before purchasing. Even the best bananas would be covered in dirt, due to being deliberately picked green and buried below ground to ripen before someone could steal them.

Our family car was a 1985 diesel four-wheel drive Toyota Land Cruiser with a "Troop Carrier" design that had inward-facing bench seats in the back—and no seat belts. My dad's dental clinic was just a ten-minute drive from home, but on Kananga's jaggedly uneven dirt roads, ten minutes was more than enough time to bonk your head on the inside roof at least once during a particularly nasty ride.

When speaking to Americans about my time in Zaïre, it's hard to explain how common it was to have hired household workers. (It's also hard to explain that my great-grandfather who immigrated from China to Hawaiʻi had five wives—but that's another story. Back to Zaïre.) In a context without standard American conveniences like kitchen appliances and supermarkets, cooking had to be done from scratch and laundry washed by hand. We had no microwave, washing machine, or vacuum cleaner. We couldn't buy frozen pizza, breakfast cereal, chicken nuggets, or fruits that weren't tropical. There were no drive-thru or take-out restaurants for thousands of miles. Our bookshelf was the library, and our backyard was the park. Without electricity, there was no air conditioning or even a store that sold refrigerated beverages, much less frozen food.

My parents employed four household staff. Tatu Mukuna (*tatu*, "father" in Tshiluba) was our cook who worked inside. Tatu Kalonda was our clothes-washer/security guard/gardener who worked outside, Tatu Buapua kept watch on overnight security, and Mamu Dinanga (*mamu*, "mother") was the nanny for my baby sister, Amy.

Lavish by local standards, our house featured amenities such as a kerosene-powered mini-fridge and battery-powered lighting in each room, courtesy of a single shoebox-sized florescent bar mounted to the wall (not the ceiling) and wired to a truck battery stashed in a scary closet somewhere. Each morning when the public water supply came on for a couple of hours, Tatu Kalonda would fill up our private outdoor water tank—the volume of about two American-sized hot tubs, elevated fifteen feet in the air to create water pressure. Tatu Mukuna baked our bread, muffins, and pies.

Like other American missionaries stationed near Kananga, our house was separated from the dirt road outside by a cement wall six feet high and lined with broken glass on top to deter thieves from entering. Since the metal gate could not be opened from the outside, Tatu Kalonda would open it whenever our Land Cruiser would announce its presence with a couple of quick horn honks. To our friends back home in Hawai'i, we were roughing it. But in Zaïre, we were rich and powerful.

When I returned to Hawai'i for fifth grade, I tried to explain life in Zaïre to my friends. When they heard about our servants and the high wall, they were in awe. "You had a cook *and* a security guard?!" they would exclaim in wide-eyed disbelief. "Your house was surrounded by walls with broken glass on top? Totally rad!" Being the missionary kid who lived in Africa made it hard to fit in at Mililani Waena Elementary School. Eventually, I stopped talking about our servants and the wall. It wasn't worth the trouble. If anything, my overseas experiences erected invisible walls between my peers and me.

Thirty years later as an adult, I still think about those concrete walls topped with broken glass. What were the conditions that made those walls necessary? And why was there such a massive economic gap between my American family and Tatu Kalonda's family, who lived under a thatched roof? In many ways, my dad's work training dentists and promoting public health was motivated by a desire to address this gap. Good intentions took us to Zaïre in the first place. My parents and the Presbyterian mission sponsoring them believed it was immoral and unfair that most Zairians had no access to the kind of healthcare available in North America. We came to bring down the walls that separated our standard of living from theirs.

Or did we?

Looking back on those three years of my childhood, I remain unsettled about living behind high walls topped with broken glass. Those walls sent an implicit message: stay away from our stuff. We're here to improve your healthcare standards but only as long as our Western standards of safety, comfort, and long-term plans are not compromised. I don't fault my parents for protecting my sisters and me. I benefited from the calm and security afforded by those walls. My parents took on plenty of risk by relocating us to Zaïre in the first place. At the same time, I'm convinced that those glass-lined walls cannot be fully understood apart from the legacy of colonialism and ongoing inequity. Even if my family lived a good, Christian life behind those walls and helped as many people as possible whenever we exited through that metal gate, it would not change the vast economic gap between us. There's no quick fix for colonialism, but its existence must still be acknowledged before we can begin to address it.

In 1990, my family was in Zaïre for the *centenaire* (centennial) of Presbyterian missions in the Congo. Grand festivities marked the occasion. I still have within my reach as I write this an audio cassette recording of the ceremony. Over the course of those one hundred years beginning in 1890, the Presbyterian Church has invested tremendous resources addressing the social, spiritual, and medical needs there. My parents were part of that effort. At the same time, it's ironic that the American system of wealth and social mobility that made my family's move to Africa possible is the same system that for centuries was built on the labor of slaves taken from Africa. There is no easy solution to repair the damage, but it can be lamented as the Bible teaches us to do. There is no quick fix for hypocrisy, but it can be confessed as the Bible teaches us to do.

British journalist Dan Snow lamented this after visiting Zaïre to report on the inverse relationship between the country's vast natural resources and persisting extreme poverty. "The Congo is a land far away, yet our histories are so closely linked. We have thrived from a lopsided relationship, yet we are utterly blind to it. The price of that myopia has been human suffering on an unimaginable scale."[5]

FINAL FOUR INTERRUPTED

To help keep our family in touch with American life during our time in Zaïre, a friend of my parents would annually send a VHS tape of the NCAA Final Four (men's college basketball tournament), which would take months to arrive. I'll never forget the time we watched the tape of 1989's NCAA Championship Game between Michigan and Seton Hall. It didn't matter that the game had taken place six months earlier. This was the pre-internet era, before you could ascertain the outcome by looking online. An evening of special entertainment for our family meant watching that VHS tape on our twelve-inch TV, thanks to the two-hour window of electricity powered by the diesel generator we shared with our missionary neighbors. As a bonus, an American missionary pilot happened to be in town that night, so he came over to watch it with us.

In a back-and-forth duel of outside shooting between Michigan's Glen Rice and Seton Hall's John Morton, the game went down to the wire. With less than a minute remaining, Rice hit a three-pointer to give Michigan the lead, only to then see Morton tie the game with a three of his own. Rice missed a potential game-winner at the buzzer, and the game went into overtime. As our family huddled around the TV, the drama of it all was mesmerizing to my eight-year-old brain. During overtime, with the game's outcome uncertain, our electricity suddenly went out; the generator had been shut off for the night. Lights out. Party over. Time for bed. We would have to wait until the next night to finish watching the tape and find out that Michigan had prevailed. Regrettably, the missionary pilot had to wait even longer since he flew out the next morning. Such suspense!

Watching basketball made me feel American, but it also reminded me of my isolation from other kids in Zaïre. I was a third culture kid caught between worlds. I wondered what it would be like to play with local kids in the neighborhood. Unfortunately, I lived behind a wall and didn't speak enough Tshiluba anyway; how could that power and privilege gap be crossed? The best I could hope for was to learn French in missionary kid school so that I could converse with Zairian adults such as Tatu Kalonda.

A dependable man in his late twenties with a wife and two kids, Tatu Kalonda was my favorite of the workers we employed. His duties included washing clothes, opening the gate, buying heavy supplies (charcoal, rice) on his bicycle, and patrolling the compound to keep out thieves. Tatu Kalonda didn't speak English and I didn't speak Tshiluba, but our common language was French. He was playful, lighthearted, and had a great sense of humor. He would always speak to me in a high voice for some reason. I could never figure out why I was being spoken to like a baby, but in hindsight I think it was because he wanted to keep our friendship on a playful and innocent level. We would talk about *le Coup du Monde* (World Cup) and African soccer legends like Roger Milla of Cameroon. Like many Zairians, Tatu Kalonda's favorite sport was soccer, and I would sometimes lure him away from his chores by asking him to show me his skills juggling a rubber soccer ball off one foot. It was from Tatu Kalonda that I learned about Diego Maradona, his favorite player. We bridged our divide through talking sports.

Tatu Kalonda and I were different in almost every way: age, race, nationality, culture, wealth, and opportunity. I can't help but think of how different his children's lives would be if they were my siblings, or how different my life would be if he were my dad. Decades have passed and I don't think of him often, but I lament the sins of my white European and American ancestors whose greed and violence created and continued such grinding poverty and inequality. But I am not off the hook either. The computer I type on and the phone in my pocket could not be manufactured without minerals from DRC. The electric car I've been eyeing runs on a rechargeable lithium battery that requires cobalt mined in DRC. I lament the sins in which I am complicit. Echoing the words of the Old Testament:

> But if they will confess their sins and the sins of their ancestors—their unfaithfulness and their hostility toward me, which made me hostile toward them so that I sent them into the land of their enemies—then when their uncircumcised hearts are humbled and they pay for their sin, I will remember my covenant with Jacob and my covenant with Isaac and my covenant with Abraham, and I will remember the land. (Leviticus 26:40-42)

May the deep suffering of this world prompt us to confess the sins of our evangelical ancestors.

A Letter to Exvangelicals

(Exploring the ways that evangelicalism has fallen short makes me all the more aware of those who have been harmed by it and as a result have left evangelicalism. I lament their losses with them and offer this open letter.)

Dear Former Evangelicals,

My purpose for writing is to acknowledge the pain, hostility, and injustice that have resulted in your departure from evangelical communities of faith. When the hashtag #exvangelical first caught my eye in 2018, I was disturbed but not shocked by the volume of responses. As story after story emerged from people hurt by evangelicalism, my suspicions were confirmed: The religious tradition in which I've spent my entire life continues to perpetuate patterns that harm its own, especially those who don't conform to certain criteria regarding gender, sexuality, politics, and theology.

Given the toxic features repeatedly cited in books, articles, tweets, and testimonies, it's understandable why you would consider leaving evangelicalism for greener pastures. What really surprised me, however, was learning how many of you actually wanted to stay. Most of you did not leave glibly or impulsively but did so as a last resort to preserve your own dignity. I'm amazed by how many of you made valiant attempts to endure until you could no longer inhabit evangelical spaces with integrity. Some of you have found new spiritual homes in mainline Protestant, Catholic, or Eastern Orthodox expressions of faith. Some of you have left Christianity altogether.

As a pastor, I'm troubled whenever I hear stories of Christians who had every intention of keeping their spiritual home in the evangelical community but were pushed out by leaders more concerned with maintaining control than reflecting "the overwhelming, never-ending, reckless love of God" we sing about in church. Instead of hearing offenders take responsibility for their wrongdoing, many ex-evangelicals have been blamed for the wounds they've sustained.

The goal of this letter isn't to lure you back or place the onus on you to fix what's wrong with evangelicalism. I want to simply acknowledge that we have done you wrong. Despite our commitment to love Jesus and live out his teachings, we have failed to treat you with dignity, respect, and love. I wrote this book in part to better understand for myself what has gone wrong so that those of us still on the inside can work to prevent future harm.

I pray that my fellow evangelicals will listen to your stories and begin to see that collective self-awareness is a discipleship issue. We can't remove the log from our own eye if we won't acknowledge that it's there. We can't cultivate a healthier evangelicalism until we understand what makes our spaces toxic to some of our siblings in Christ.

As we listen and learn from your stories, may we hear the Spirit speaking through the pain and work to be people who leave a better space behind.

PAIN AT THE PALACE

Tour guides and travel websites often describe 'Iolani Palace as "the only official royal residence in the United States."[6] This unique fact makes it a popular attraction for visitors, but it also raises questions: How did the royal palace of an independent monarchy located over 4,800 miles away from Washington, DC, become property of the United States? Was it purchased, surrendered, or released with consent?

To say that Hawai'i is home to the only royal palace on US soil sounds exotic, but this reduces an enduring injustice to an item of trivia. After learning that Hawai'i's government was illegally overthrown in 1893 by businessmen (among them children and grandchildren of American missionaries) backed by the US Marines, another way to put it would be, "Of all the treasures stolen from indigenous peoples in the nineteenth century during the United States' imperial conquest from sea to shining sea and beyond, 'Iolani was the only royal palace they stole."

In 1895, Queen Lili'uokalani was arrested and forced to abdicate her throne. She endured a public trial before being sentenced to imprisonment in a former upstairs guestroom of the

Palace for nearly eight months. In the Imprisonment Room, she was denied all visitors except for one lady companion.[7] When US President McKinley sent a proposed Treaty of Annexation to the Senate in 1897, thousands of Hawaiian Kingdom citizens rallied against it, submitting petitions protesting and ultimately preventing its ratification. However, in spite of clear resistance from Native Hawaiians and non-Hawaiians alike, the United States went ahead and annexed the islands by a joint resolution of Congress in 1898, foregoing the protocols set forth through international law.[8]

In 2019, our summer InterVarsity group visited 'Iolani Palace as part of Ho'olohe Pono, an annual intergenerational immersion into Native Hawaiian communities to listen, learn, and serve with the love of Jesus. With its ornate Victorian era furniture and towering portraits of monarchs, the palace might look like a museum when viewed through Western eyes, but for Kanaka Maoli (Native Hawaiians), this is sacred ground. For those of us non-Kanaka in the group, the palace felt like a collection of opulent relics from the distant past. The more artifacts in a given room, the longer it took to explore. As I would learn that day, this is not how everyone experiences 'Iolani Palace.

While our contingent shuffled slowly through the tour at a pace regulated by docents monitoring our every move, I noticed some from our group moving further ahead. They were gathering near the emptiest room's entrance, waiting for the docent to let them proceed. Instead of lingering in the rooms full of furniture, these friends of mine, most of them Kanaka Maoli followers of Jesus, wanted to spend time in the Imprisonment Room. It wasn't that the other rooms didn't matter. They just wanted to be where their queen had been incarcerated. Perhaps they knew something about being occupied in their own homeland. After all, Jesus did too.

Seeing my friends' tears as we walked through the palace taught me more about how the past shapes the present than any docent or audio tour recording. It also showed that injustice doesn't need to have the last word. The places of deep loss can also be places where hope arises.

My friend Moanike'ala Nanod-Sitch elaborates:

Apahu'a (the land where 'Iolani Palace sits) holds the tears of our people. It holds the injustices, but also the hopes, joys, and celebrations of our people. From this *'āina* [land] our prayers rise up and *ke Akua* [God] hears them. . . . Even before 'Iolani Palace was built, our *kūpuna* [ancestors] loved and sought ke Akua in this place. Our people have come here to remember, weep, and mourn for our stolen nation, for what our queen and kūpuna endured, and for the pain that our people and land continue to endure. We also come here to stand for what is *pono* [right, just, fair for all] in response to these injustices with hope and inspiration from the *'onipa'a* [steadfastness] and faith of our kūpuna as they trusted in *Iesū* [Jesus]. What was missing from the tour is the *piko* [navel, umbilical cord, center, source] and the heart. We especially remember what took place when we come to the queen's room. She cried out to ke Akua on behalf of her beloved people but also prayed for mercy upon those responsible for our suffering. We come to this space to listen, not just out of love for land, but love for nation. When we weep together in the queen's room, we're calling out to ke Akua in lament, and with the question in our hearts, "Queen Lili'uokalani, how did you do it?"[9]

One of the songs Liliʻuokalani wrote during her imprisonment is "Ke Aloha o ka Haku," translated "The Lord's Mercy." It is also known as "The Queen's Prayer." In it, she forgives her captors and points us to *Iesū* who did the same. Knowing what took place on this sacred ground, it's an appropriate response to cry out: Jesus, come and heal! Come and restore what has been desecrated by sin, evil, and idolatry. Help us, Lord!

The church is broken in so many ways. Systemic injustice is a discipleship issue that harms the body of Christ. We need God's Spirit to heal the wounds and restore the broken places. And how we get there is through repentance.

7

LEARNING TO REPENT COMMUNALLY

MY WORLD CHANGED when my parents' mission work transferred us from Kananga, Zaïre, to Kathmandu, Nepal. Beginning in the seventh grade, I attended an international Christian school that was also much bigger (forty students) than the one I attended in Zaïre (twelve students). In Kananga, most of the other missionary kids were like me—US passport holders. This was not the case in Kathmandu, where Americans were a minority among foreigners. In my seventh grade class of nine students, three of us were from the United States. The others were from the United Kingdom, Canada, the Maldives, and Nepal.

Being in the minority, I developed friendships with peers who weren't interested in American sports. I learned to refer to football as *gridiron* or *American football*, not just because the rest of the world uses the word *football* for soccer but also because there is *Aussie rules football* and *Canadian football*. I learned about the British Columbia Lions as well as the New Zealand All Blacks—who are actually a rugby team, but you get the point.

Even though we all lived in Nepal, it was clear that we had arrived there from very different places. Most of the time, the competitive subtext between countries manifested itself in joking remarks about the differences between our passport countries. We argued playfully about whether to call the alphabet's last letter *zee* or *zed*. We joked about the spelling of *colour*, *programme*, and *centre*. We traded barbs on how to pronounce *sorry* and *about*. *Math* or *maths*? *Restroom* or *washroom*?

Thankfully, my Canadian friend Ian and I shared an interest in baseball, so at least we could talk about the World Series— even though it doesn't actually represent the world. It helped that the Toronto Blue Jays were major league champions twice in the early nineties. (Notice that I avoided saying *world* champions.) If we weren't talking baseball, Ian and I would find other ways to pit the United States against Canada, like the time we debated whether American or Canadian Olympic sprinters used more steroids. There we were, two North American sports junkies in the Himalayas.

Without many Americans around, something strange happened. I found myself gravitating to badges of American identity. It's almost unthinkable in retrospect, but I became the missionary kid who loved all things red, white, and blue. I took pride in being a US citizen. In a country without McDonald's, Doritos, or Mountain Dew, what was an adolescent boy to do? When my friends had nothing good to say about my passport country, I felt a responsibility to represent the United States in those conversations if I was the only American present.

Looking back on it, I reached for my American identity in Nepal because I felt like an outsider among outsiders. It was the latest link in a chain of events that began when I moved from Hawai'i to Canada at age six, from Canada to Zaïre at age seven, from Zaïre back to Hawai'i at age ten, from Hawai'i to Kentucky at age twelve. Once again, I found myself in new surroundings, a half-white, half-Chinese American in Central Asia, attending an international school that followed the British educational system. Since I clearly wasn't Nepalese, British, Canadian, or Australian, the appeal of claiming my American-ness grew stronger than ever. Like a mountain climber who loses their footing and starts sliding downward, I grabbed hold of the closest sturdy object within reach: American citizenship. It wasn't because I thought the United States was superior to other countries or that we were God's chosen people but because I needed an identity that wasn't going to change every three years. I began collecting American artifacts to stabilize my sense of belonging: T-shirts, magazines, and cassette tapes of pop music. I had to know there was a home for me somewhere . . . anywhere.

Staying current with American pop culture while living half a world away required great effort in the pre-internet age. Having already experienced what it was like to re-enter the United States after living abroad, I knew this transition would eventually happen again. I wanted to be prepared for that. My parents bought me a subscription to *Breakaway* magazine, published by Focus on the Family, as well as *Sports Spectrum* magazine, which featured articles about professional athletes who were Christians. It didn't matter that they took months to arrive. In a bizarre turn of events, I was living the life of an American evangelical teenager but in the Himalayas!

Relics from the United States were hard to come by. Without a reliable system for international mail delivery, the only way for a teenager to acquire such merchandise was either to ask my parents to have a coworker purchase and pack it inside their precious luggage space or to bring it back myself after visiting the United States, which we did every other year. I'll never forget the time I requested a three-by-five-foot American flag. True story. When it finally arrived, I hung it on my bedroom door so that everyone would know they were entering American territory. All I can do is facepalm in reminiscence. There I was, the biracial kid from Hawai'i living in Kathmandu with the Stars and Stripes boldly displayed on his bedroom door.

During this period, I also tried my best to collect Christian T-shirts—evangelical ones to be precise. These were hard to come by in Kathmandu, so I only remember having two. The first one said "go against the flow" with a Jesus fish swimming the opposite direction from all the other fish. The other one was my favorite: an American flag–themed T-shirt, the design wrapped from front to back against a faux-denim background. On the front were the words of 2 Chronicles 7:14, "If my people, who are called by my name, will humble themselves and pray and seek my face and turn from their wicked ways, then I will hear from heaven, and I will forgive their sin and will heal their land."

I think this T-shirt was my favorite because it integrated two aspects of my identity that mattered most to me at that time: Christian and American. With its stonewashed red and blue print peppered with irregularly shaped white stars, the shirt was also reminiscent of the US national soccer team's similarly garish uniforms worn during the 1994 World Cup.

Though I longed to be a typical American teenager, my up-bringing taught me that Christianity did not begin in the United States, nor is American evangelicalism representative of the global body of Christ.[1] My school in Nepal was staffed by Christian teachers who shared an evangelical ethos, yet in addition to expatriate missionary kids like myself, I also had classmates from Hindu, Buddhist, and Muslim families seeking an international education. Whenever my family visited the United States, I was struck by how superficial and sheltered my peers seemed to be. At the same time, I envied them. It wasn't until my re-integration into American society during college that I noticed how my up-bringing gave me a unique perspective on evangelicalism.

By the time college began, I knew there was no universal version of church, only geographic variations. Having lived outside the United States for the better part of a decade, between ages seven and eighteen, I understood that when I attended a church service in Illinois, it was Illinois-flavored Christianity being practiced there. When our home church in Hawai'i switched denominations in order to preserve (read: pursue) a more conservative doctrinal outlook, I understood this as one of many churches leaving one of many denominations for another. When a Wheaton professor joined the Catholic Church, I was surprised and intrigued but not horrified. I didn't yet know where I would land on the denominational spectrum (college freshmen rarely do); the varieties of Christian belief and practice prepared me to assess the strengths and weaknesses of American evangelicalism.

CULTURAL TOOLKITS

If I were to pick one characteristic that distinguishes the American flavor of evangelicalism from other varieties, it

would be the assumption of individualism, especially in predominantly white communities of faith. In their classic study-
turned-book, *Divided by Faith*, sociologists Michael O. Emerson
and Christian Smith describe the notion of a *cultural toolkit*, a
repertoire of "ideas, habits, skills, and styles" that "creates ways
for individuals and groups to organize experiences and
evaluate reality."[2] Jemar Tisby believes white evangelicals' cultural toolkit helps explain how Christians of different racial
backgrounds often have such different views on contemporary
social concerns. Tisby says that "differing toolkits applied by
black and white Christians help illuminate some of the conflicts over racial justice."[3] Three tools in this kit are worth
noting here:

1. *Accountable individualism*, which holds that "individuals exist
   independent of structures and institutions, have freewill,
   and are individually accountable for their own actions."[4]

2. *Relationalism*, which sees social problems as fundamentally due to broken personal relationships.

3. *Antistructuralism*, the belief that "invoking social structures
   shifts guilt away from its root source—the accountable
   individual."[5]

Taken together, these three seemingly innocuous assumptions have contributed to the major shortcomings described in
the previous chapter. Every culture has its own toolkit. There's
nothing wrong with having one. The problem starts when your
cultural lens isn't named for what it is: *a cultural lens*. It's one
thing to say, "This is how things look from my vantage point." It's
another thing to say, "I'm not describing my vantage point. I'm
describing the complete truth as is true for everyone." Because

of hyperindividualism, Tisby says, the white evangelical main-stream "tends to reduce the importance of communities and institutions in shaping the ways people think and behave."[6] Thus we are prone to the consequences stemming from thin ecclesi-ology, propensity for schism, celebrity dependence, and capitu-lation to idolatry. When repentance from sin is always preached as something individual and never collective, the Bible's robust paradigm of repentance gets reduced into something much nar-rower. In the book, *Forgive Us: Confessions of a Compromised Faith*, the authors assert,

> Most evangelicals acknowledge that every person has sinned, but evangelicals often fail to recognize that sin exists well beyond the personal level. [The apostle] Paul's emphasis on the universality of sin suggests that we should also be aware of the power of corporate sin. Nowhere, in fact, does Scripture ever reject the idea of corporate sin, and yet we frequently find just such a rejection in the history of the evangelical church in America.[7]

DID JESUS REPENT?

Jesus' example of being baptized by John offers a blueprint for collective repentance as God's people.

> Then Jesus came from Galilee to the Jordan to be baptized by John. But John tried to deter him, saying, "I need to be baptized by you, and do you come to me?"
>
> Jesus replied, "Let it be so now; it is proper for us to do this to fulfill all righteousness." Then John consented.
>
> As soon as Jesus was baptized, he went up out of the water. At that moment heaven was opened, and he saw the

Spirit of God descending like a dove and alighting on him. And a voice from heaven said, "This is my Son, whom I love; with him I am well pleased." (Matthew 3:13-17)

Why would a sinless Jesus respond to John the Baptist's invitation to "repent and be baptized"? If there was ever anyone who did not need baptism for the forgiveness of sins, it was Jesus. John the Baptist understandably did a double-take and tried to stop Jesus, saying, "I need to be baptized by you, yet you come to me?" Jesus responded, "Allow me to be baptized now. This is necessary to fulfill all righteousness."

How does Jesus' baptism fulfill all righteousness and justice? It depends how we approach the concept of righteousness. If it's just about individual moral perfection, there's no need for Jesus to be baptized. But if it's about the repentance of his people, then Jesus, as a member of the community, needed to be included for corporate repentance to take effect. Jesus acted in solidarity with his people, including their baptism for repentance. One of my seminary professors puts it this way:

> Jesus assumes Israel's sins as his own. He says yes, we are still living the consequences of our unfaithfulness to our God as his people, and I'm part of that people. So in baptism Jesus joins Israel in preparing for the imminent work of God to bring Israel through the end of its suffering for sin and into the new life that God has long been promising. How Jesus is in solidarity with Israel's suffering and sin is central to what it means for him to be Messiah, son of David, son of Abraham.[8]

Jesus didn't seek baptism because he thought he was guilty of individual sin. Jesus understood himself as more than an individual person. He was a member of his community, a people who needed to repent. In that sense, Jesus did not view the sins of his people as anything other than his own. If Jesus participated in corporate repentance for Israel's sins, how much more should modern-day evangelicals?

THE PROBLEM WITH "NOT ALL . . ."

Let's say the city of Los Angeles wanted to make a concerted effort to reduce air pollution, a shared problem that affects all residents. Given that Los Angeles is a space with millions of inhabitants who would all benefit from cleaner air, it makes sense to measure the air quality and determine the primary causes of contamination. Appropriate questions would include the following: How bad is the problem? Who is most affected and how can we best address the situation? In this scenario, the focus would be on making a shared space healthier for its residents.

But what if instead of measuring air quality and pinpointing causes, the city emphasized that *not all* Angelenos are contributing to the problem. What if the city divided residents into two categories, good and bad? Those deemed "good" Angelenos might assume that their car emissions and energy usage weren't related to the issue. They would be absolved of responsibility and thereby disincentivized from reducing their carbon footprint. The city would have a harder time reducing the air pollution because some people wouldn't be contributing to the solution. By saying "not all residents," the city would be undermining its own message that everyone has a part to play and that all Angelenos breathe the same air. Each inhabitant of this shared space is affected, regardless of whether they are deemed "good" or "bad."

In a similar way, when we let a select group of evangelicals off the hook, we lose sight of how evangelicalism is doing as shared space. The impulse to say #notallwhitepeople or #notallevangelicals tends to deflect responsibility away from a privileged group of so-called good white people and so-called good evangelicals, as if individual residents can be separated from the place where they reside. This can minimize essential aspects of the entity in question, whether whiteness or evangelicalism. When we say, "Not all of us are bad," we create a loophole through which people can assert that they're not part of the problem. This shifts the paradigm from collective space back to individual brand. By saying "not all . . . ," the emphasis turns toward a distinction we've created between two new categories of people (good white people and bad white people), instead of focusing on the shared effect of a common element in question, in this case, whiteness. Similarly, if we're trying to ascertain what evangelicals need to repent of as a whole, let's not be too quick to distinguish between good and bad evangelicals. Scripture teaches that *all* have sinned and fall short of God's glory (Romans 3:23). All of us are complicit in ways we don't always see or understand. The deeper issue has to do with the features that make evangelicalism the space that it is.

ROTTEN TO THE CORE?

With all that's gone wrong and continues to go wrong, it's fair ask if evangelicalism is rotten to the core. How deep do our problems go? Some would say they go so deep that all the water in evangelicalism's well has been thoroughly poisoned beyond redemption. If this is the case, an appropriate response would be to treat evangelicalism as a disaster zone and evacuate as many to safety as possible. Depending on how you've been treated in evangelical spaces, I can understand why some would leave it all behind and urge others to do the same.

Since I'm in the camp that sees evangelicalism as *mixed* with poison rather than *pure* poison, I don't believe it's beyond repair. That said, I'll grant that there are times when leaving evangelical spaces is the best course of action. If you are under an abusive leader or have experienced serious trauma at the hands of evangelicalism, you may have to leave evangelicalism in order for your faith in Jesus to survive.

Sandra Maria Van Opstal agrees that white evangelical culture can be toxic for Latina pastors like her, yet she senses a call to remain. "I'm staying in my evangelical family with the hope that we can be reformed," she writes. "My desire is that the communities that have historically been overlooked, marginalized, or intentionally ignored will be given a place of honor. I am here to remind my family that the global church has moved from the west to the south."[9] Van Opstal goes on to say that the barriers her community faces motivate her to speak out rather than leave. "Evangelicalism is about conversion, reform, transformation, and repentance," she contends. "If I'm going to remain, I'm going to use my voice for reform. I'm going to take seriously how the authoritative Word of God speaks to the racism and xenophobia of our evangelical family."[10]

WHAT TO DO VERSUS WHO TO ASK

Those who have been wronged know better than anyone what it will take to make things right. This is true for both the individuals and groups currently being harmed by structures of evangelicalism. Good things happen when the question shifts from, "What should I do?" to "Who should I ask?"

The caveat here is that marginalized people are not responsible for educating the privileged. The onus is not on the oppressed to teach the oppressor. However, if a question arises from a genuine desire to center those who have been historically marginalized, then asking questions can be a way of finding out what it will take to make things right.

Mark Charles and Soong-Chan Rah write, "Individual sins like lying, sexual assault, theft, and even murder can be addressed by the American church as it offers Christ simply as a personal Savior. However, the need to address corporate sins like stolen lands, broken treaties, genocide, slavery, sexism, systematic injustice, white supremacy and Christendom itself is ignored or outright rejected."[11]

Practices of repentance will vary according to the type of sin and ensuing damage that was done, but our focus here addresses *how* to help evangelicalism repent more than providing a complete list of *what* we should be repent from. Whether we're talking about our sins against African Americans, indigenous people, immigrants, or LGBTQ+ persons, the ones who have been being wronged know better than anyone else what it will take to make things right. Let's listen not only to their stories about pain and injustice but to their recommendations for how to make it stop.

We can't eradicate systemic patterns of sin overnight, but we can confess our complicity and cry out for God's liberation.

Instead of trying to compile an exhaustive list of sins to confess, I invite you to take note of the damage that's been done in your context. As we develop the habit of confessing evangelicalism's transgressions in collective terms, we'll be better positioned to learn from our mistakes and make right what has gone wrong. Confession constitutes a key practice for inhabiting evangelical spaces faithfully.

PRACTICAL STEPS

Here are some ways to cultivate repentance in evangelical contexts:

1. Take note of the damage. Where has the fabric of shalom been torn? If you are new to learning about the situation, your role is to listen to those who have been harmed, not sit in the judge's seat evaluating how bad the damage is.

2. Develop the habit of confessing transgressions in collective terms. Word choice is important in collective repentance, especially plural pronouns like *we, our,* and *us.* This requires that we acknowledge both *proximity* and *complicity.*

   After the shooting death of Laquan McDonald by a Chicago police officer, pastor Daniel Hill prayed at a vigil, "We repent of the violent acts done in the name of racism. We repent of the apathy that has caused so many of us to sit on the sidelines. . . . [We repent for] the history of holding our people, our color, our kind as the epitome of most valuable, and of devaluing so many other people. Of devaluing so many black lives."[12] Hill received hundreds of vitriolic emails, angry tweets, hate mail, and even death threats from fellow white people. But Hill's corporate prayer of repentance follows the biblical pattern of lament.

3. Cry out for God's liberation, individually and corporately. The shift from sinner's to sinners' might only be a matter of infinitesimal punctuation, but it makes a world of difference. May we teach one another to pray sinners' prayers and not just a sinner's prayer.

4. Be part of the solution. Learn from others with more experience than you. Be willing to take risks and make mistakes. Start with small steps and increase them over time. Join the Holy Spirit's work of making right what has gone wrong.

Part IV

RENEWAL

8

IS EVANGELICALISM
WORTH RENEWING?

LANCE GAVE HIS LIFE TO JESUS at a summer youth camp.[1]
The friends he made there became his first community of faith.
Over the next two years, Lance became more active with the
Christian organization that ran the camp. In this evangelical
space, he grew to love studying the Bible and having deep
conversations about life's ultimate meaning. As he experienced
the joy of walking with Jesus, Lance actively shared his faith with
peers at school, eventually becoming a small group leader and
someone his peers looked up to in the fellowship.

Like most evangelical parachurch ministries, the youth organization believed in sexual abstinence outside of marriage. To
promote this, leaders reinforced the unofficial tenets of *purity
culture* including the idolization of virginity, marriage and sex as
the reward for chastity, men as lust machines, and women as

responsible for the purity of men.[2] Dating and physical contact with the opposite sex were prohibited at all youth events. Lance found these rules somewhat restrictive, but he generally adhered to them because his faith was a priority and he wanted to be a good example for his small group.

When Lance started college, he felt drawn to the possibility of becoming a pastor but wasn't sure if this was part of God's plan or merely his own desire for recognition and influence. He geared his studies toward the health care industry, training to become a radiology technician while also joining a nondenominational church plant near the college. He continued volunteering with the parachurch youth ministry that had been so formative yet also noticed how restrictive it felt compared to his new church.

With his pastor's encouragement, Lance's church involvement grew into a more established role on the tech team. He was loving it. Part of what made this church plant exciting was the pastor's authenticity in narrating his own spiritual journey, which had been through some deconstruction but had since been rebuilt with an ethos that encouraged people to question their previous religious assumptions. "The old way of doing church no longer works," Lance's pastor would say, "but the future is a place where churches will focus more on asking the right questions than giving the right answers." Nothing seemed off limits to discuss or challenge, which contrasted with Lance's youth ministry background, where voicing doubts and questioning authority were discouraged.

Lance's attention to detail made him effective in the medical field, but at church he began noticing inconsistencies that didn't add up. His pastor's sermons touted the value of question-asking, but behind the scenes, some topics were still taboo. Over the next two years, the church grew rapidly from a small operation into a more established congregation, a change that Lance embraced initially, though he missed the open-ended atmosphere of the past. With the church preparing to launch its next church plant, the pastor's patience for big questions waned as his focus became increasingly business-minded and goal-oriented. What was once an outside-the-box community of authenticity had become just another conventional church focused on its own programs. Lance didn't realize it at the time, but this was his first experience of significant disappointment with a mentor in ministry.

As Lance prepared to graduate from college, it was revealed that one of his former youth leaders from the parachurch organization had sexually abused a minor student. Other stories of emotional and spiritual abuse began to leak out. Lance couldn't make sense of why God would allow this to happen. What if the people who led him to Christ were frauds too? Lance's theological questions had grown bigger, but his church's capacity to address them had shrunk. The gray areas that used to feel boundless and energizing were now a source of conflict and resentment for Lance. He began wondering if his pastor's inability to supply satisfying answers was due to the bankruptcy of Christian theology.

The more time that passed without a place to process his questions, the more Lance lost hope in the power of the Christian story. The easiest place to vent was social media, which led to cantankerous debates with self-appointed doctrinal gatekeepers who lacked pastoral skill and compassion. It didn't happen all at once, but eventually Lance decided he was done with the church. Far from being an easy process, it was a painful loss of his spiritual home. But since evangelicalism was the only form of Christianity that Lance had ever known, his departure amounted to leaving the faith. He has not attended church since.

LESSONS FROM LANCE

What can evangelicalism learn from Lance's story? I would contend that the contexts of an evangelical church and parachurch ministry are more than incidental to what happened. Although the outcome wasn't inevitable, a case can be made that evangelicalism's flaws played a part in Lance losing not only his personal faith but also the soul-nourishing resources of his Christian community. Let's take them each in turn:

1. *Celebrity dependence*: Like many growing evangelical churches, Lance's congregation centered around a magnetic leader on whom the church's fortunes rose and fell. When the pastor's vision changed, Lance experienced ill-timed disappointment with a mentor who became so focused on church growth that he could no longer shepherd Lance through the dissonance. Since the youth ministry and church plant both fostered an atmosphere of striving for numeric benchmarks, sometimes at the expense of emotional health, Lance didn't have role models for how to slow down and develop spiritual practices like Sabbath, stillness, and solitude. Lance's faith was an indirect casualty of an evangelical culture that elevated doing at the expense of being.

2. *Thin ecclesiology*: Without an ecclesial structure beyond his local church, Lance wasn't offered sufficient resources to develop his faith stream awareness. Since he was conditioned to expect that the church's purpose was to support his personal spiritual life, Lance had little use for the

church once it stopped meeting his individual needs. Furthermore, the church plant's lack of affiliation with a broader entity resulted in a missed opportunity to glean wisdom and support from a more established congregation, which could have reduced the risk of Lance falling through the cracks as his church experienced rapid growth and changed from being open-ended to program-driven.

3. *Propensity for schism*: Faced with contradictory church experiences that he couldn't reconcile, Lance did what evangelical culture trained him to do: he went shopping for a church that agreed with his views. Some of them were okay, but even small annoyances with those churches triggered negative reactions in Lance stemming from unprocessed grief over how things ended with his pastor. Lance interpreted his pastor's lack of capacity to provide satisfying answers as widespread deficiency across Christianity as a whole. This all-or-nothing dichotomy contributed to his rejection of the church.

4. *Complicity with idolatry and injustice*: The only theological options modeled for Lance were the rigid purity culture of his youth group and the contrasting inconsistent open-endedness of his pastor. Once Lance lost trust in his youth organization's integrity, his faith underwent some deconstruction with little guidance on how to reassemble it back together. He did his best to seek answers, but since he lacked a supportive faith community to help make sense of his disturbing observations of failed leadership, it wasn't long before social media interactions with combatively opinionated Christians stoked enough cynicism for Lance to spiritually check out.

APPROACHING RENEWAL COLLECTIVELY

Having looked at awareness, appreciation, and repentance, we come to the fourth posture for grappling with dissonance about the evangelical church: renewal. Everything covered so far converges here. Our renewal efforts will be more effective when practiced in concert with the first three postures. After cultivating faith stream awareness, gaining appreciation for our strengths, and learning repentance from our sins, it's time to take action for change. If you skipped ahead to this chapter, go back and learn the first three postures. You'll be much better prepared for the work of renewal if you're already pursuing awareness, appreciation, and repentance. Faith stream awareness puts you in a better frame of mind to pursue renewal. Appreciation gives you tools for renewal work. Repentance removes barriers to healing and tills the soil in which renewal can take root.

Approaching evangelicalism in individualistic rather than communal terms makes it harder to take responsibility for a shared space. This is especially true if we don't consider other evangelical sub-groups part of our spiritual family. We might wonder why we should even care about denominations besides our own. What's the point of investing energy in groups we don't belong to or theologically agree with? Interestingly enough, even the most individualistic evangelicals have some experience with thinking in communal terms. Anyone who cares about the well-being of their particular church, Christian school, or ministry organization has entered the realm of taking ownership of a shared space. If we can think collectively about the concerns of our local neighborhood, our profession, or even something as large as the country where we live, why not begin taking responsibility for evangelicalism as a shared space?

When an oil tanker malfunctions and dumps petroleum into the ocean, someone must clean it up. Even if the ocean doesn't return to its previous state, there's an urgency to contain the damage to prevent it from spreading further. But when evangelicals make a mess, who cleans it up? When evangelicals inflict harm, who is held accountable? We can't undo the situation or return things to their previous state, but we can stop the damage from spreading and clean things up to prevent future harm. Without renewal, sinful patterns will continue unacknowledged and unaddressed. Evangelicalism will become less inhabitable for many who desire to live here. On the other hand, a renewed evangelicalism means less abuse, less ignorance, less injustice, less arrogance, and fewer embarrassing scandals. Beyond reducing harm, renewal also makes it possible for evangelicalism to become more of what God intends it to be: a vibrant body of Jesus' disciples characterized by the Spirit's fruit: love, joy, peace, patience, kindness, goodness, faithfulness, gentleness, and self-control.

Approaching renewal collectively begins with conversations about how to clean up the mess where we're able. The mess is too big for any one person to tackle alone, but it's okay to start small. Join a book club. Encourage a disillusioned friend. Pray for your church's leaders. Use a Bible translation that doesn't use "men" when it means "people," or "brothers" when it means "brothers and sisters."[3] Revise your Christmas carol lyrics, especially the second and third verses of "Hark the Herald Angels Sing," so that "pleased as man with men to dwell" becomes "pleased with us in flesh to dwell," "born that man no more may die" becomes "born that we no more may die," and "born to raise the sons of earth" becomes "born to raise each child of earth." These examples aren't earth-shattering, reminding us that the steps toward renewal can be small at first. Don't let the big picture keep you from taking little steps.

WHAT RENEWAL IS NOT

Before going deeper into what renewal is in chapter nine, let's clarify what it is not. Renewal is not about making cosmetic changes to mask a lack of real change. To renew something means to make it better, which requires changing it in some substantial way. Therefore, renewal is not simply about rebranding the status quo so that it's more palatable and presentable. If evangelicalism's problems run as deep as this book describes, superficial and decorative changes will fail to leave things in a better condition than we found them. Renewal cannot be more of the same.

The reason why this matters is because too often evangelicalism becomes preoccupied with bolstering its own poll numbers. We judge ourselves based on how successful we are at drawing crowds and presenting a likable image. In our desire for followers, we work very hard at maintaining a reputation that doesn't turn people off.

Our reasons for renewing evangelicalism should not be about restoring some kind of former glory or reasserting a position of cultural prominence and proximity to power. This is not renewal. On the contrary, true renewal is about being transformed into the likeness of Christ, not only as individuals but as a beloved community inhabiting a shared space.

WHY RENEW EVANGELICALISM?

If, in after practicing the first three postures of awareness, appreciation, and repentance, you're still interested in sticking around to make evangelicalism a better place, congratulations! You get to join the work of renewal. Simply put, renewal for evangelicalism is the work of leaving a space better than you found it. Renewal makes it a more gracious, sustainable, just, and spiritually healthy place to live. Since the well-being of evangelicalism's residents matters to God, it is for their sake that we strive to improve conditions for both current and future community members who follow Jesus.

Personally speaking, one of my main motivations for renewing evangelicalism is to reduce harm and toxicity. Too often, I have seen people involuntarily removed from evangelicalism despite the fact that they wanted to stay. Most of these removals are unnecessary. My heart breaks for people who wanted to stay evangelical but weren't allowed to.

In the name of maintaining doctrinal purity, evangelical culture can be prone to knee-jerk reactions that result in excessive actions taken against those who don't conform. But kicking people out of evangelicalism is usually counterproductive. By removing someone from their spiritual community, we sever vital connections between Christians and the soul-nourishing resources that evangelicalism offers. We must learn to do a better job of disagreeing and even disapproving when appropriate but without having to needlessly expel people or cut off relationships. It's one thing for someone to conclude they'll be better off in another faith stream besides evangelicalism. It's another thing for someone to be displaced despite wanting to retain evangelicalism as their spiritual home.

A second reason to renew evangelicalism: it gives people hope. In 2010, our second son, Vincent, died of a liver tumor at the age of eighteen months. In the weeks and months that followed, my wife, Rebecca, and I were very open with our grief, albeit in different ways. Rebecca wore her pain like a badge on her sleeve—at least that's how it felt to me. When we would meet new people, she would make sure that our deep loss was one of the first things they knew about her. If you couldn't handle that subject, she wasn't interested in being your friend. I, on the other hand, processed my grief through writing blog posts on special days so that friends and family from around the world could share in our experience. When meeting new people in person, however, I was very careful not to bring up the topic unless there was a measure of trust where I felt safe enough to disclose such painful and vulnerable details about our son.

After a year of writing monthly blog posts about Vincent and my grieving process, I no longer felt the need to post as frequently about him on social media. I learned other ways of honoring his memory that didn't feel so public. I would still post something for his birthday and the anniversary of his death but without feeling the weight of keeping his memory alive. If casual friends of mine forgot about Vincent, that was okay, because I knew that those close to us would not. Furthermore, I began noticing that sharing my story of grief and disappointment with God gave others hope. People have shared that my honesty and realism about what we've been through helps them face their pain, doubts, and struggles. Some people have even given church another chance because of how the evangelical community walked with our family through this valley.

Unfortunately, I've also seen the consequences of congregations who have done a poor job acknowledging the devastating heartache and doubt that often accompany deep loss. When an evangelical faith community pressures those who are hurting to declare victory too soon, it backfires. Instead of fostering hope and resilience, the minimization of struggle can end up feeding cynicism and despair. This results in more unnecessary damage that could have been prevented. On the other hand, when evangelicals step up to do what the community of faith did for our family, hope increases all around. By holding together faith and doubt as compatible partners, our evangelical friends and family imparted hope to carry on. That's why renewal matters. A healthier, less toxic evangelicalism means more hope and spiritual resilience overall.

A third reason to renew evangelicalism: to reflect God's heart instead of the empire's values. God would have his people be humble and healing rather than proud and divisive. Paul's reminder to Corinth remains timely for North American evangelicals: "For though we live in the world, we do not wage war as the world does. The weapons we fight with are not the weapons of the world. On the contrary, they have divine power to demolish strongholds" (2 Corinthians 10:3-4). Pursuing a liberated evangelicalism involves nothing less than an exchange of worldly weapons for God's divine power—the kind that overcomes evil with good. Just as an individual disciple cannot follow Jesus without being challenged and changed, so, too, must a community of faith be continually transformed as it adapts to the present times and context. When evangelicalism is a healthy space, newcomers find it inviting and are more likely to consider making it their spiritual home. A renewed evangelicalism glorifies God and points us toward the New Jerusalem where "God's dwelling place is now among the people, and he will dwell with them" (Revelation 21:3).

Finally, renewal matters so that we will be a credible and compelling witness to the world instead of an embarrassment or cause for repulsion. Renewal is needed in every part of evangelicalism that promotes idolatry or perpetuates injustice. In Jemar Tisby's words, "Christianity became identified with the emerging concept of whiteness while people of color, including indigenous peoples and Africans, became identified with unbelief."[4] Wouldn't we rather be known for telling the truth so that healing can begin? By seeking renewal for our corner of evangelicalism, we participate with God in the renewal of all things. One of my denomination's mottos implores Christians to be people who live intentionally "for God's glory and neighbor's good."[5] May that be true of how we go about the work of renewing evangelicalism.

CAVEATS FOR RENEWAL EFFORTS

As you approach the task of renewal, be mindful of the pitfalls that come with such efforts. One of these is the illusion that it's always better to fix something than to start over. This is not true. Sometimes it's more effective to create new spaces rather than invest in existing structures that are past due or overripe.

For example, Jemar Tisby writes about this regarding seminaries, but it applies to other organizations too. He notes the advantage of starting new schools with a diverse board of trustees, faculty, and staff. Rather than trying to add diversity, racial and ethnic variety would be built into the foundation. Sometimes it's just not possible to "tweak existing structures enough to adequately educate their students in a culturally responsive way."[6] Therefore Tisby concludes, instead of expending valuable energy transforming a school whose personnel may resist the very idea of anti-racism, that energy could go toward starting a new seminary that is already racially aware and responsive.

Second, renewing evangelicalism is not an invitation to prove that we're better than the old evangelicalism. Yes, we want to improve things, but it's not a competition. Returning to the oil spill metaphor, the goal of cleaning it up is for the sake of the ocean, not the glory of the cleaners. We do it to make the ecosystem healthier, not to showcase our own prowess. When creating new spaces, it's better to view them as part of the renewal process rather than as a way to score victories for our brand. When evangelicals get territorial about their market share, we miss opportunities for new growth, creativity, and sustainable innovation. I've noticed a pattern of new church plants inadvertently launching due to a conflict or fallout with their parent church, rather than as communities lovingly birthed through an intentional process of healthy multiplication. We cannot completely prevent others from feeling threatened by the start of new initiatives, but at the same time, the posture of renewal is best pursued when we recognize that every Christian denomination or network has an interest in cultivating a healthier evangelicalism.

One last caveat for renewal is to keep expectations realistic. No matter how many dreams become reality, new problems will arise too, so we can't expect perfection. Mistakes are inevitable. The goal isn't to arrive at flawlessness but to move in the right direction. Even if we're moving slowly, this is still better than moving in the wrong direction. We can't let the fear of failure hold us back. Again, Jemar Tisby says it well: "Standing for racial justice involves risk. But effective advocacy is a skill just like any other, and skills can be learned. Ultimately though, you cannot read your way, listen your way, or watch your way into skillful advocacy. At some point you must act."[7] Renewal requires action.

FORGETTING OUR LOOKS

The author of James writes about the importance of not merely listening to the Word but doing what it says:

> Anyone who listens to the word but does not do what it says is like someone who looks at his face in a mirror and, after looking at himself, goes away and immediately forgets what he looks like. But whoever looks intently into the perfect law that gives freedom, and continues in it—not forgetting what they have heard, but doing it—they will be blessed in what they do. (James 1:23-25)

For evangelicals, the journey of renewal includes remembering what we've seen in the mirror of "the perfect law that gives freedom." As evangelicalism's dirty laundry continues to make headlines, let's not forget our looks. I hope we'll remember what we saw along the journey through awareness, appreciation, and repentance. May we do more than survey the problem. Let's stop giving lip service to change but instead live differently in light of what the mirror has shown. In order to make the changes necessary for renewal, we cannot forget our looks.

WHEN EVANGELICALISM BECOMES TOXIC

During my freshman year of college, a guy who lived on my floor converted from evangelical to Eastern Orthodox. After learning about the Orthodox Church in a theology classes, he shared his enthusiasm with whoever would listen. Whenever I'd see him in the hallway, he would share something he valued about Eastern Orthodoxy that had been lacking in his experience with evangelical Christianity. One week it was the smell of incense and the sound of bells. Another week it was the apostolic lineage that traces back to the early church. Since I hadn't even heard of the Orthodox branch of Christianity (some would call it "the trunk") at that point in my life, I remember feeling perplexed as to why this guy was so excited. I assumed he was using the word *orthodox* to mean having correct beliefs. I was glad that he found a church with correct beliefs, but this didn't seem like something to write home about. It wasn't until later on that I appreciated the magnitude of his decision and the shift it represented. I now see this as a positive example of someone who left evangelicalism for another place on the Christian map after finding that it would be a better context in which to follow Jesus.

Leaving one's faith stream is a big decision not to be taken lightly. Just like there are good ways and bad ways to leave a local church, the same is true of a faith stream. It's particularly unwise to depart rashly or without fully considering the implications of your choice. Why not at least take stock of the benefits being left behind? Evangelicalism can be a very life-giving place for some, but others have experienced too much pain and are barely hanging on. I'm reluctant to say that evangelicalism should be vacated wholesale, but I'm also someone who personally would have much to lose by leaving. Some danger zones are more susceptible to harm than others, but it's still people's spiritual home. Returning to the geographic metaphor, if people can make their home in a desert or frozen tundra, people can make their spiritual home in evangelical spaces.

A growing number of evangelicalism's former residents—reflected in the hashtag #exvangelical—are voicing their reasons for leaving. Some have departed because of a spiritually toxic environment. Others were kicked out for differing too much from dominant norms. Whether their departure was voluntary or not, these ex-evangelicals remind us that evangelicalism isn't a healthy space for all of its residents.

One prominent voice from the ex-evangelical movement is Chrissy Stroop, editor of the book *Empty the Pews*, named after the hashtag that she started.[8] In the book, Stroop describes in painful detail her journey of being rejected, harassed, and slandered for not fitting the paradigms expected of her by American Christians. Skeptics of books like *Empty the Pews* may try to minimize the problem by rationalizing that people are leaving because of their own unwillingness to play by the rules. We might not want to pay attention because it's painful to read stories of people who have left the church. One key feature of being an evangelical involves believing that following Jesus and remaining faithful to him is a matter of urgency. Because of that urgency, it can be difficult for evangelicals to accept when someone we love chooses to walk away from the faith. What I find even more tragic in such situations is how many of these stories of being rejected and cut off did not need to happen.

JESUS IS BIGGER THAN EVANGELICALISM

My heart breaks when people equate evangelicalism with the totality of Christianity. What happens when evangelicalism is no longer a healthy place for them to inhabit? If we teach our flock that rejecting evangelicalism amounts to rejecting Jesus, we have deceived our own people. Moreover, we have sown seeds into the lie that if someone doesn't want to be part of evangelicalism, there is no place for them in Christianity.

I understand that every church makes mistakes. Every community of faith and parachurch ministry goes through times when they fail to demonstrate the grace and love of our Savior. This does not mean we have a monopoly on Jesus. It is so tragic to me when someone leaves the Christian faith without ever visiting a non-evangelical church. Jesus is so much bigger than evangelicalism. The New Testament was not written by English-speaking, evangelical Protestants any more than your high school teacher wrote *Romeo and Juliet*. We are but stewards of a living story that each new generation re-tells in its own style. Modern evangelicals may trace our heritage to the early church, but that makes us no different from other Christian streams who do the same thing.

My plea is that if you know someone who is considering dropping out of Christianity because of their experience with a narrow pocket of evangelicalism, make sure they know the difference between the two. Evangelicalism is not homogenous. It varies greatly by race and geography. Anglicans and Baptists both follow Christ but with different approaches. Their respective visions for how to train clergy, disciple their members, and celebrate the Lord's Supper are full of contrasts. That's why awareness matters so much for renewal. When evangelicals perpetuate the myth that their little group has exclusive access to Jesus, the Bible, the Holy Spirit, or, heaven forbid, the one true God in three persons, we cause spiritual damage that someone else will have to clean up.

It might be too late to bring back those who have moved on, but we can still do our part to take collective responsibility for this place called evangelicalism, not only to benefit current inhabitants but also future generations who will live here. Just as we have a responsibility to care for rainforests, coral reefs, and freshwater lakes for the sake of those who come after us, let's steward evangelicalism well enough for our spiritual children and grandchildren to live out their faith here.

9

BETTER THAN WE FOUND IT

IT WAS 1999, MY SENIOR YEAR of high school at Faith
Academy in Manila, Philippines. Australian singer-songwriter
Paul Colman visited the campus to perform in chapel for students, then later for an evening concert attended by the wider
community of missionaries. I only remember three details about
that concert. First, I couldn't get over how cool it was that
Colman's percussionist simply played a single snare drum with
brushes and an egg shaker. Second, upon returning home that
night, I remember trying in vain to mimic Colman's strumming
patterns on my acoustic guitar. Third, I'll never forget the
moment when he was heckled by a parent in the audience.

Between songs, Colman mentioned that God loves us tenderly
like a mother caring for a newborn baby. He observed that the
Bible sometimes describes God using feminine imagery such as
a mother comforting her child (Isaiah 66:13) or a hen gathering
her chicks (Luke 13:34). Colman even brought up the fact that

God doesn't actually have a gender since God isn't a creature confined to human categories.

At that point, a woman in the back of the auditorium shouted loud enough for all to hear, "But God is our Father!" The room's atmosphere intensified sharply into sheer silence. You could have heard a pin drop. Colman was initially taken aback, but he took the interruption in stride, agreeing with a smile that yes, the Bible describes God as our Father too. He could have left it there and started his next song, but instead he chose to restate his original point: masculine and feminine metaphors for God can both be appropriate because God is neither male nor female. Nobody objected. Everyone took a collective breath in their seats, then it was onward to the next peppy tune.

This interaction may have taken place in Southeast Asia, but the majority of the room's audience was North American evangelicals. Reflecting on that moment, I'm struck by how it illustrates an ongoing tension within evangelicalism over matters of gender-based roles rooted in theological assumptions that conflate masculinity with God's essence. It's rare to hear evangelicals overtly declare that God is male, but this erroneous idea is assumed and implied by the resistance to anything other than male metaphors or pronouns for God. I have no idea if any minds were changed by Colman's words that night, but I do know that everyone at the concert was listening when he affirmed and reaffirmed feminine imagery for God from the platform. I believe the work of renewing evangelicalism happens in moments like these.

Renewal is more of a posture to continually adopt than a threshold at which to arrive. The goal isn't to reach perfection or eliminate all flaws. It's more about moving in the right direction, doing so continually over time. Or goal in cultivating evangelicalism's renewal is not to return to a bygone era but to leave this space better than we found it. Evangelicalism will always leave behind scars, but hopefully we can reduce the number of open wounds.

RESISTING TRIUMPHALISM

As much as I'm tempted to call for an all-out push to move full speed ahead with renewal, I cannot truthfully do so with integrity. I care deeply about evangelicalism's future, but of the four postures this book proposes, renewal is the one I'm most hesitant about. It's not that I'm cynical about renewal—at least not all the time. My concern is triumphalism, which says: our faith stream deserves to dominate the landscape. Evangelicals have historically been quick to declare victory. Our eagerness to make direct contact with God comes with a dark side. From altar calls to child sponsorship sign-ups, we prize objectives that can be achieved before people head for the parking lot. When we reach these goals, we high-five ourselves for getting things right and helping others find the truth. Talk of renewal can open the door to triumphalism. I would even say that whenever the topic on the table is evangelicalism's renewal, the danger of triumphalism isn't far off.

Let's return to our environmental metaphor. Should we champion the reuse of glass bottles or reduce our consumption of single-use plastics? Well, yes and no. It's a good thing to reduce, reuse, and recycle as much as we can. The problem is attaching a certain meaning to these actions. If we think we have arrived at environmental responsibility simply by treating plastics differently, we have taken a step in the right direction, but we still have a long way to go. As good as carbon neutrality is, the goal isn't to reach a point where we as individuals are free and clear of our responsibility to the earth. The goal is to care for all of creation and love our (future) neighbors by leaving the earth in better shape than we found it.

In the same way, we won't arrive at a fully healed and renewed evangelicalism on this side of heaven. Instead of being motivated by a desire to get ourselves off the hook, let's make the most of this opportunity to give the gift of a welcoming and soul-sustaining environment for evangelicalism's future inhabitants. A healthy awareness of evangelicalism's mixed legacy will help to keep us humble. According to Jemar Tisby, "American Christians have never had trouble celebrating their victories, but honestly recognizing their failures and inconsistencies, especially when it comes to racism, remains an issue."[1]

Before we get to some practical steps that cultivate renewal, it's worth pausing to consider not only *how* to do it but *who* should lead those renewal efforts. What can we learn from the people evangelicalism has harmed? If renewal is defined as bringing something back to its original condition of freshness and vigor, I can see how some ex-evangelicals might object to the notion that evangelicalism's original condition is worth pursuing in the first place. After all, when was evangelicalism ever in pristine form, uncorrupted by its vices of hyperindividualism, racism, and sexism? I can also see how sexual minorities might ask, "When was it exactly that evangelicalism treated us well? Which past version of evangelicalism is worth returning to?"

These are reasonable questions. There's a danger to the idea that we should seek to gain back the power evangelicalism has lost. For example, when we ignore evangelicalism's historic complicity in racism, we risk returning to an evangelicalism that views only some people as made in God's image. Tisby reminds us, "White evangelists compromised the Bible's message of liberation to make Christianity compatible with slavery."[2] While there are certain elements from the past that evangelicals should appreciate and conserve, there are sinful patterns we should not perpetuate. Glamorizing an evangelicalism of yesteryear does not move us forward with integrity. Let's not fuel the nostalgic notion that evangelicalism's best days are behind us. With all the harm we've done in Jesus' name, I pray that those were not our best days!

RESISTING CYNICISM

In addition to triumphalism, there's an opposite danger: cynicism. We shouldn't minimize what has gone *wrong*, but let's also not minimize what has gone *right*. If evangelicalism is a mixed bag, then by definition it's not all bad. Giving up hope for evangelicalism altogether would miss opportunities to join God in the renewal of all things—even this thing called evangelicalism. Rebecca Solnit writes, "Hope is an embrace of the unknown and the unknowable, an alternative to the certainty of both optimists and pessimists. Optimists think it will all be fine without our involvement; pessimists take the opposite position; both excuse themselves from acting."[3] With God's help, may we avoid the paralysis of cynicism.

VISION OF A RENEWED EVANGELICALISM

Imagine the effect of a renewed evangelicalism. Instead of assuming centrality for ourselves, we would acknowledge our unique faith stream. Instead of splitting off into increasingly narrow theological niches that suit our doctrinal tastes, we would appreciate the evangelical heritage we share in common. Instead of kicking the misfits out, we would welcome them in. If we learned to leave evangelicalism better than we found it, it could become a space marked by the postures of awareness, appreciation, repentance, and renewal.

A renewed evangelicalism would be marked by faith stream awareness, where we acknowledge our vantage point. By recognizing our own embeddedness in culture, we would recognize the importance of both giving and receiving hospitality.

A renewed evangelicalism would be marked by appreciation for our heritage, where we celebrate what our forebears have passed down to us. We would have roots in orthodoxy but branches in innovation, as Fuller Seminary likes to say.

A renewed evangelicalism would be marked by true repentance, where we wouldn't just say the right thing but live the whole gospel of Jesus. The authors of *Forgive Us* put it this way: "It would be easy to blame the racists and sexists in the Christian community and distance ourselves from them. But we must begin to see the corporate responsibility that the church holds in our presentation to the world. How do we contribute and perpetuate the public wrongdoing of Christians through our silence and passivity?"[4] In a renewed evangelicalism, followers of Jesus have the integrity to name the idolatries and injustices that plague our spiritual home, and we take meaningful steps to make right what we've done wrong.

A renewed evangelicalism would foster community transformation rather than toxicity and marginalization. We would continue to invest in the aspects of our space that are doing good work, while also supporting new work that fills the gaps of what's missing from the landscape, such as Jemar Tisby's idea for starting a new seminary with diversity in its DNA.

CULTURE CARE FOR EVANGELICALISM

To illustrate how to cultivate renewal, allow me to build a metaphor on someone else's metaphor. Acclaimed artist Makoto Fujimura, in his book *Culture Care*, proposes that we take care of our culture with the same urgency that we care for the earth's environment. He believes we need to protect cultural resources such as noncommercial art, as if it was an endangered forest or coral reef that can't be replaced.

Like a bountiful ocean polluted by toxic waste or a vibrant forest exploited by commercial interests, societal forces threaten to reduce beauty and creativity to utilitarian commodities. When we treat the earth primarily as a means for monetary gain, we can permanently damage its capacity to be a life-giving habitat for humans and animals. The same is true when we treat artistic beauty as solely a money-making tool. "Just as we are learning the importance of taking care of our environment to leave the earth healthy for future generations," Fujimura writes, "so we must all care for culture so future generations can thrive."[5] *Culture Care*'s core message is that beauty is as vital to society as clean water is to the earth.

Just as the environment's misuse is often sanctioned by a utilitarian ethos that values commercial production at the expense of ecological integrity, the commodification of beauty makes corresponding sacrifices at the altar of economic prosperity. In unwavering opposition to such forces, Fujimura declares, "Culture is not a territory to be won or lost but a resource we are called to steward with care."[6] If beauty faces a predicament parallel to the biophysical world's climate crisis, culture is in no better shape than creation.

Let's apply the metaphor of culture care to evangelicalism. I propose that we learn to protect and care for evangelicalism's resources with the same conviction that underscores our care for the physical world. For an increasing number of Christians, evangelicalism is becoming uninhabitable because we keep polluting its spiritual water supply with idolatry and injustice. When its integrity is compromised, evangelicalism becomes more known for making souls sick than for making them well.

Visualizing evangelicalism as a living environment helps us to pinpoint areas and entry points where the work of cultivating a healthier evangelicalism can begin. A good place to start is where we see parts of evangelicalism's ecosystem that need healing and renewal. Conversely, if we identify something about the evangelical living environment that is worth affirming, continuing, and spreading, let's invest resources to cultivate appreciation for that aspect. The better we care for our spiritual habitat, the more likely it will remain intact for future generations. How might we care for our local corners of evangelicalism?

Nobody expects deforestation or water pollution to be reversed quickly. Even those whose lives are dedicated to environmental protection recognize the need for long-term sustainability in their efforts. Part of the work involves changing personal habits, such as reducing electricity consumption by turning off lights and appliances. Another aspect includes policy reform, such as creating incentives for those who save power. In a similar way, the task of making evangelicalism a more habitable space calls for individual actions as well as policy change. Most of what has gone wrong stems from idolatry or injustice. Let's keep that in mind as we look for entry points to join the work of renewal.

ONLY THE PRIVILEGED?

As a middle class, cisgender heterosexual male who is married and has two graduate degrees, I recognize that I write from a position of privilege. Given the benefits I'm afforded by my gender, education, races (white and Asian), socioeconomic status, sexual orientation, and US citizenship, it's fair to ask if renewal is an endeavor reserved for evangelical elites. The luxury of assessing evangelicalism as a broad entity assumes a privileged vantage point to begin with. My guess is that if you're reading this book, your life may share a lot in common with mine. How does the work of renewal apply to less powerful evangelicals in the pews who want to keep it simple and get to the bottom line? How do we respond to those who say, "Instead of worrying about how well evangelicalism is doing, can't we just focus on following Jesus and leave it at that?"

I absolutely agree that we should follow Jesus in practical ways that are accessible to folks who don't read books about evangelicalism. To prevent evangelicalism from becoming a country club for insiders, privileged folks like me must continually learn from newcomers to this space and the evangelists who invited them here. Following Jesus from any and every social location is a hallmark of evangelicalism. The work of cultivating healthier spaces is not reserved for those who can articulate its historical and theological contours. You don't need to understand the ozone layer to protect the environment. You don't have to know the periodic table of elements to reduce air pollution. Similarly, making our churches and ministries healthier does not require a grasp of evangelicalism's inner workings. The postures of awareness, appreciation, and repentance will spur us toward renewal. Anyone who inhabits evangelicalism and practices these postures can learn to make it a healthier space.

"EXCEPT THE WOMEN"

One of the ways I cultivate renewal is by advocating for women leaders in ministry. By giving encouragement, affirmation, and advocacy for gender equality, I strive to leave evangelicalism in better shape than I found it. My wife, Rebecca, is a pastor who has been a trailblazer in the area of helping people see that God does in fact call women to shepherd the flock. Why else would God gift so many of them with pastoral abilities and vocations?

One of the ways that we have pursued renewal in this area is by sharing books and resources that provide theological support for women in ministry. Bestowing these treasures and fostering adjacent conversations help people gain new insights and go deeper in their discipleship.

Over the course of our married life since 2003, Rebecca has been employed by several different congregations belonging to denominations that hold a complementarian perspective. In one church, she was the first woman to preach since Corrie ten Boom passed through in the 1950s. In another congregation, she was the first woman to *ever* preach on a Sunday morning. Following Rebecca's first sermon there, a woman in the congregation approached her with tear-filled eyes and very few words. All she could say was, "This is new for me." In that moment, God was broadening the scope of what she thought was possible.

Cultivating a healthier evangelicalism isn't a task for heroic lone rangers. Things work out better when we pursue the vision together. Systemic change takes time—and takes a lot out of those who challenge existing structures. That's why it's important to approach evangelicalism realistically as a mixed bag.

One year as a birthday present for our lead pastor, we gave him the book *Man and Woman, One in Christ* by Philip Payne.[7] After reading it, our pastor's viewpoint began to shift. This is no small thing in a denomination that does not ordain women pastors. However, we have seen fruit in the years since: women in his congregation now perceive themselves as capable of being called by God to serve in church leadership.

I don't share this example to congratulate myself but as a practical way that God has worked through us to bring about change on a small scale within our context. Despite evangelicalism's ongoing flaws, including patriarchy and male-centered paradigms, our little corner of evangelicalism is being renewed in this area by God's grace. As a result, we desire and trust that God will work through these changes to foster a more balanced representation of gender in church leadership positions at all levels.

Having said that, let's remember that egalitarians are not immune to sexist assumptions and actions, especially those of us who are egalitarian men. Even with the best of intentions and strongest of convictions, men still see the world through male lenses. I'm reminded of the time in seminary when Rebecca and I both took a course on Matthew's Gospel from one of our favorite male professors who we know to be a strong supporter of women in ministry leadership.

One day in class, our professor probed the crucifixion's deep significance, his written lecture reaching a crescendo adorned with haunting imagery and thick irony. Having reached the moment when the cross becomes Christ's coronation ceremony, our professor described Jesus as the final king of Israel, heir of God's own power. "Betrayed by his own people's authorities and even from within his inner circle," he declared, "there is nobody clean of responsibility. The disciples had all left him. Jesus was abandoned by everyone."

At that point, Rebecca, one of four women in a class of twenty, interrupted our dearly loved professor's beautifully crafted lecture to say, "Except the women." The professor paused his reading, nodded in agreement, and repeated her words "except the women" before launching into an unscripted ode to the faithfulness of Jesus' female disciples. This story reminds me that renewing evangelicalism will take more than men who believe the right thing. Without the leadership and insight of women, we'll remain stuck in a male-centered rut.

PRACTICAL SUGGESTIONS

How do we inhabit evangelicalism in ways that leave it better than we found it? Here are some practical ways:

- Name particularity. Instead of perpetuating evangelical normativity by disparaging other expressions of Christianity, we refer to evangelicalism by its specific name. This places evangelicalism in proper context as one of many locations on Christianity's big map. Jesus is much bigger than evangelicalism.

- Adopt realism. Rather than succumbing to cynicism about evangelicalism on one hand or strident idealism on the other, we adopt a realistic posture that acknowledges both its beauty and its brokenness. This helps us navigate the complexity of evangelicalism as it truly is, including the ways it falls short of our ideals.

- Lament corporately. As God's people did throughout Scripture, we confess the sins our community has committed. We grieve ongoing patterns of wrongdoing that harm communities treated as expendable. We take collective responsibility for our particular corners of evangelicalism but with an expanded view of confession, repentance, and discipleship that includes evangelicalism as a whole, not just individual persons, churches, and organizations.

- Talk less about the brand, more about the space. We acknowledge evangelicalism's diverse global landscape instead of perpetuating caricatures of an exclusively American political brand on which to pass judgment. If we decide to continue inhabiting evangelical spaces, we invest in its well-being so that future generations can experience abundant life in Christ here.

- Listen to ex-evangelicals' stories of how and why they left, whether voluntarily or involuntarily. If you can find an ex-evangelical who is willing to share their experience in front of a group, this could be an incredibly valuable way to learn how to improve. The only caution with that is not to further traumatize the person by blaming them for the pain they feel or criticizing them for their perspective.

- Look to the margins. Prevent unnecessary departures by doing "early intervention" at the first sign of cynicism or ostracism. This could take the form of educating people about faith stream awareness or introducing them to other Christian streams besides evangelicalism.

- Speak up. When you see your fellow evangelicals perpetuating harm, especially with good intentions, do what you can to correct them and stop the damage. Imagine a sinking boat that's taking on water. Some respond by using buckets to empty the water and buy themselves more time. But what if while this was happening, nobody noticed a misguided person using their bucket to *add* more water to the boat? Surely it would be worthwhile, for the sake of the whole boat, to inform them of the harm they're causing and redirect them to use their bucket to work in concert with those *removing* water.

- Keep the onus off those being harmed. It's not the job of victims to fix perpetrators. When you see someone lashing out at evangelicalism, help them to feel heard. Don't underestimate the effect of spiritual abuse or actual trauma they may have endured.

- When attending an evangelical gathering of any kind, notice the demographics of who is leading, not just who is present. If the vast majority of gatherings you attend are led predominantly by white males, look for evangelical initiatives and ministries led by women and people of color.

- Use your platform. Raise awareness and call attention to changes that need to be made.

Church Clarity is an example of a resource that cultivates healthier evangelical spaces by helping visitors ascertain a church's policies on women in leadership and LGBTQ+ participation.[8] Whether your church's theology of human sexuality is closer to "side A" (the view that God blesses same-sex marriages) or "side B," (the view that same-sex attracted Christians are called to celibacy),[9] Church Clarity believes it is reasonable for those who are most affected by the policy to have accurate information in order to make an informed decision as to whether that church aligns with their beliefs. To accomplish this, Church Clarity's database publishes church scores (such as "clear" or "unclear") based on how well their websites communicate actively enforced policies on questions like whether a given church officiates same-sex weddings or if women can serve as elders. An analogy here would be food ingredients used at restaurants. If someone is a vegetarian, they have stronger reasons to know the ingredients than omnivores do. A friendly server or welcoming atmosphere are insufficient reasons to expect the vegetarian to enjoy your restaurant. Without some key facts about your food, good intentions can actually cause more harm. By closing the ambiguous gap between what a church's website says and which policies are enforced, Church Clarity fosters greater consistency regarding the practical outworking of a church's theological claims.

GLIMPSES OF HOPE

Every posture brings glimpses of hope. Whenever we get discouraged about the state of evangelicalism in our context, we can still ask, What gives me hope for evangelicalism today?

Awareness: It gives me hope when our men's group at church discusses political difference in a civil and relational manner. These conversations would not be happening without an evangelical church providing the space to host it. It's not that these conversations couldn't happen outside the church, but because of their mutual respect for one another coupled with the commonly shared essentials of faith, this group inspires me with hope that our disagreements don't have to dissolve friendships within the church.

I'm inspired by Robert Webber's actions to initiate the "Chicago Call: An Appeal to Evangelicals" in 1977. Webber saw that evangelicals lacked historical consciousness, but he wasn't content to leave things that way. He not only envisioned a healthier evangelicalism, he rooted that vision in the best of what evangelicals bring to the table: a love for the gospel in all its fullness. The solution he saw wasn't to become less evangelical but more—even to the point of saying, "We cannot be fully evangelical without recognizing our need to learn from other times and movements concerning the whole meaning of [the] gospel."[10]

Appreciation: The faculty at Fuller Seminary hail from a multitude of denominations across the Protestant spectrum. What gives me hope is not only the theological diversity paired with unity around Jesus but the way I've seen faculty relate to one another. Being a fly on the wall for jovial theological exchanges between Kuyperians like Richard Mouw and Anabaptists like Erin Dufault-Hunter is worth the price of admission. They chide each other about their traditions' differences but always find ways to express appreciation for what the other's tradition brings.

Repentance: At Urbana 18, I experienced hope during the time of lament. I expected it would be a spiritually heavy time, which it was, but it also showed the power of naming what we've done and allowing God to transform it.

Renewal: Every summer since 2006, InterVarsity Christian Fellowship in Hawai'i has organized an event called Ho'olohe Pono, which means "to listen well or to listen intently for what is just." This event gives me hope for the renewal of evangelicalism because it empowers Native Hawaiian leaders to show us a better way.

What gives you hope today?

HOPE FOR YOUR STRUGGLE

SOME RESTAURANTS CARRY TOO many options on the menu. If you want to eat a sandwich, you probably don't need nineteen choices to find one that will satisfy. Whatever you select for the middle will still be surrounded by bread on both sides. Other restaurants have the opposite problem: not enough choices. One vegetarian entrée. Two kinds of dessert, both smothered in fudge sauce. Nothing dairy-free.

Both scenarios present challenges, but when it's time to place your order, you're better off with too many choices than with too few. If you can't decide between several options that all sound good, you'll probably still enjoy eating whichever selection you make. However, if there's nothing on the menu you can actually envision yourself eating, it might be time to consider finding another restaurant—if that's even an option.

I hope this book has helped you know that when it comes to your spiritual life, you have options. Depending on your situation, you might have more options than some or less than others. Whether you decide to remain with evangelicalism or not—or make changes later on—my hope is that you're in a better position to make informed decisions about where to put down roots. These four postures of awareness, appreciation, repentance, and renewal can be cultivated in other faith streams too. Inhabiting evangelicalism as your primary spiritual habitat might not work for you anymore, which is okay. There's still hope in your struggle because, like all creative chefs, God will provide options for you.

The framework I've suggested isn't a cure-all for ambivalence but a pathway for struggling well. Or at least better than before. Each posture can be adopted one at a time or they can be cultivated together in harmony. If you know someone who feels like they've run out of options with Christianity, consider which posture could be life-giving to them. Share what has helped you. Teach these postures to your classmates, students, and children!

I don't expect evangelicalism to stop making headlines anytime soon. As you encounter more stories of mistreatment by evangelical institutions and their leaders, your heart will break again. You're not alone in lamenting evil cloaked in spiritual language. As events unfold that further expose evangelicalism's sins in the public eye, it's quite possible that you'll continue grappling with the magnitude of what it all means and your place in it. Whatever the future holds, it's better to have too many choices than too few.

Heavily invested as I am, I still feel like leaving evangelicalism sometimes, even if it is my home. Writing this book hasn't ended my struggle. Reading it may not end yours either. Although my quest for belonging continues, I'm thankful to have a better handle on what it takes to struggle through the reluctance that

Dr. Erin articulated so well. Her words are worth repeating once more for those in the back:

> Just as I did not choose my blood family, I did not decide who would also come into this space of open gifts of grace and peace through Christ. . . . Despite our sometimes tense and important divergences, we are all claimed by the good news of what God has done in Christ, enticed by what God reveals in Scripture, and invigorated by the Spirit for engagement with a creation beloved by the One who created it.[1]

Wherever you are in the struggle, God is there with you. When you don't know where "home" is, God is still with you. Even when you're in the middle of the stream and don't know which way to go, God is still with you.

Let's keep the conversation going as we grow in our capacity to cultivate awareness, appreciation, repentance, and renewal.

ACKNOWLEDGMENTS

THIS BOOK WOULDN'T EXIST without a village of amazing people who each made a difference through their prayers, insights, stories, feedback, guidance, encouragement, and other sugars that made the medicine go down. Thank you for responding when I cried out, "HELP!"

I am especially grateful to: my unshakable editor, Al Hsu, for your legendary mix of skills, which brought out the best in what I wanted to say.

Rich Mouw, for your gracious foreword and even more gracious friendship.

The incredible folks at IVP, for accepting my proposal and turning this dream into reality. It was a joy to work with Rachel, Lori, Krista, Tara, Maila, and Elissa.

Missio Alliance, for opening a two-thousand-word door in 2017 that slowly grew into this book.

Elisabeth Licitra, for your impeccable photography, capturing my best angles since 2013.

My fabulous launch team and generous endorsers.

Indispensable writing companions: Chuck Liu, Wendell Au, Cheryl Wallick, Jan Avellana, and Kenneth Chang.

Conversation partners who sharpened my ideas: Mark Licitra, T.C. Moore, Cathy Rubasch, Karen Jolly, Jerry Romasco, Chandra Crane, Brennan Takayama, Joe Thackwell, Gideon Mbui, Jean Carlos Arce, Steven G. Henderson, Victor Hsiao, Mike Karim, Jeanne Keuma, Jason Floyd, Chris Romine, JR Rozko, Lauren Grubaugh, Steve Chun, Jarrod Phipps, Morgan Pōmaikaʻi Lee, and Brian Flora.

Encouragers who believed in this project: Daisy Yoshimura, Greg Ehlert, Rachel Kuo, Lori Gregg-Hammer, Kalei Hosaka, Leah Hosaka, Stacey Breshears, T.J. Breshears, James Puleo, Brenda Wong, Terry Lock, Stephanie Nelson, Susannah Kandikatti, and Michele Turek.

Scholars who provided invaluable expertise: Dani Espiritu, Jane Hong, Hunter Farrell, Daniel D. Lee, Love Sechrest, and Randy Furushima.

Communities who supported me during the writing process: Wellspring Covenant Church (especially the prayer team), InterVarsity GFM West (most notably the Pacific and SoCal area teams), my IV Hawaiʻi ʻohana, the grad students and faculty of UH Mānoa, Kapiʻolani Community College, and USC, the saints of St. Anthony Retreat Center, Kailua Community Church, Pasadena Covenant Church, Christ Our Savior Church Chicago, River of the Valley/Rio del Valle, and faithful ministry partners around the globe.

Gifted shepherds who led me to green pastures and beside still waters: Tim Tseng, Janna Louie, Lisa Liou, Dale Vallejo-Sanderson, Cheryl Takabayashi-Foo, Perry Alexander, and Lito Guimary.

Wise mentors and guides who restored my soul: Suzanne Shaw, June Naughton, Mike Harbert, Ken Fong, Jay Jarman, and Ada Lum.

Courageous teachers who led me in paths of righteousness and justice: Moanike'ala Nanod-Sitch, Erin Dufault-Hunter, Tommy Givens, Lisa Sharon Harper, Kathy Khang, Joy Moore, and Makaiwa Kanui.

My family who keeps my cup overflowing: Theo, Andre, Mom, Cheryl, Blake, Amy, Jon, Norman, Linda, Esther, and Yoon.

Finally, Rebecca, thank you for everything. No human being did more to keep me going. This book is your baby too.

DISCUSSION QUESTIONS

**INTRODUCTION: WHEN EVANGELICALISM
IS YOUR MOTHER**

1. What's your reaction to the idea of the church as your "mother?" How has your relationship with Christianity shaped and nurtured who you are today?

2. How familiar are you with inhabiting evangelical spaces, past or present? What has it been like for you to inhabit those spaces?

3. To what extent and in what contexts do you identify as an evangelical Christian? Is it helpful to distinguish between the evangelical brand and evangelicalism as a space?

CHAPTER 1: STRUGGLING WITH EVANGELICALISM

1. Do you resonate with Dr. Erin's description of a "reluctant evangelical"? Why or why not?

2. Are there any parts or characteristics of evangelicalism that make you feel at home? If so, what are they?

3. Which is harder for you: grappling realistically with evangelicalism (not expecting too much from it) or redemptively (not expecting too little)?

CHAPTER 2: DEFINING EVANGELICALISM: UNDERSTANDING OUR HISTORY

1. Of Du Mez's four ways of defining evangelicalism (theological category, cultural movement, white religious brand, diverse global movement), which have you encountered most? Least?

2. When evangelicalism is reduced to a brand, which inhabitants of evangelical spaces get left out?

3. Of the four ways that evangelicalism the brand differs from evangelicalism the space, which contrast stands out to you most: politics versus religion, white American versus multiracial and global, consumers versus inhabitants, or individual versus collective mindset?

CHAPTER 3: FAITH STREAM AWARENESS: KNOWING YOUR LOCATION

1. What faith stream(s) have shaped your spiritual journey? What are some of the key features that come to mind?

2. Which benefit(s) of faith stream awareness do you find most compelling and why?

3. Do you agree with the author's list of evangelicalism's strengths and weaknesses? What might you add or change?

CHAPTER 4: WHY APPRECIATION MATTERS

1. How has evangelicalism impacted you in a positive way?

2. Using the metaphor of evangelicalism as a family of origin, what do you appreciate about the traits or emphases it passes down?

3. How might something that you consider to be a strength of evangelicalism be seen as a weakness by others?

CHAPTER 5: STRENGTHENING OUR STRENGTHS

1. How easy is it for you to appreciate evangelicalism's strengths? If it's difficult for you, what might be some reasons for this?

2. What steps could you take to practice appreciation through fostering the kind of collective memory encouraged in Scripture?

3. Which book(s) by evangelicals of color do you plan on reading and why?

CHAPTER 6: EVIL CLOAKED IN SPIRITUAL LANGUAGE

1. Where or when have you seen Christianity being complicit with injustice, exploiting the vulnerable, or perpetrating evil cloaked in spiritual language? Which "sins of the ancestors" come to mind as needing to be confessed? (Leviticus 26:40)

2. Reflecting on the concept of repenting communally for collective sins, what might it look like to broaden your prayer life from individual repentance to include more collective expressions of confession and repentance?

3. What area(s) of deep suffering in the world prompt you to confess the sins of evangelical ancestors? As you think of those affected, are they located predominantly inside the church, outside it, or both?

CHAPTER 7: LEARNING TO REPENT COMMUNALLY

1. Can you identify the cultural lens(es) that have shaped your faith experience? What are some possible shortcomings that accompany this perspective?

2. What stands out to you about the solidarity Jesus expresses at his baptism (Matthew 3:13-17)? What would it look like for you to identify with the sins of your people?

3. How deep do you think evangelicalism's problems go? As you consider learning about how to make things right, who comes to mind as a resource?

CHAPTER 8: IS EVANGELICALISM
WORTH RENEWING?

1. What's your reaction to Lance's story? How did evangelicalism's characteristics as a space contribute to the outcome?

2. When evangelicals make a mess, who have you seen cleaning it up? Where do you feel drawn to join the ones cleaning it up, even if it means starting small?

3. Think of someone (it could be yourself) who has left evangelicalism due to it being an unhealthy space to inhabit. Was this break inevitable or were there circumstances that, if handled differently, could have prevented the loss of a spiritual home?

CHAPTER 9: BETTER THAN WE FOUND IT

1. Which do you see as a larger obstacle to renewal: triumphalism or cynicism?

2. Do you think renewal is a posture reserved for evangelical elites? If so, why is this the case? If not, what is the role for "ordinary" evangelicals in the process?

3. If you plan to stay with evangelicalism, what steps can you take to leave it better than you found it? From where will you draw inspiration and hope to persevere in this challenging work?

NOTES

INTRODUCTION: WHEN EVANGELICALISM
IS YOUR MOTHER

[1]Pew Research Center, "Orthodox Christianity in the 21st Century," November 8, 2017, www.pewforum.org/2017/11/08/orthodox-christianity-in-the-21st-century/.

[2]Lifeway Research, "3 in 5 Evangelicals Live in Asia or Africa," March 2, 2020, https://lifewayresearch.com/2020/03/02/3-in-5-evangelicals-live-in-asia-or-africa/.

[3]I will use DRC, Zaïre, and the Congo interchangeably throughout the book.

[4]Lifeway Research, "Many Who Call Themselves Evangelical Don't Actually Hold Evangelical Beliefs," Dec 6, 2017, https://lifewayresearch.com/2017/12/06/many-evangelicals-dont-hold-evangelical-beliefs/.

[5]Mark Labberton, letter to the editor, *L.A. Times*, August 26, 2017, www.latimes.com/opinion/readersreact/la-ol-le-trump-evangelicals-white-supremacy-20170826-story.html.

[6]Christopher B. Hays, personal post on Facebook, November 9, 2016.

[7]Katelyn Beaty, "I Was an Evangelical Magazine Editor, but Now I Can't Defend My Evangelical Community," *Washington Post*, November 14, 2016, www.washingtonpost.com/news/acts-of-faith/wp/2016/11/14/i-was-an-evangelical-magazine-editor-but-now-i-cant-defend-my-evangelical-community/.

[8]Sandra Maria Van Opstal, "Remaining to Reform" in *Still Evangelical? Insiders Consider Political, Social, and Theological Meaning*, edited by Mark Labberton (Downers Grove, IL: InterVarsity Press, 2018), 123.

[9]Van Opstal, "Remaining to Reform," 125.

[10]Sarah Eekhoff Zylstra, "1 in 3 American Evangelicals Is a Person of Color," *Christianity Today*, September 6, 2017, www.christianitytoday.com /news/2017/september/1-in-3-american-evangelicals-person-of-color -prri-atlas.html.

[11]Aleksandra Sandstrom, "If the US Had 100 People: Charting Americans' Religious Affiliations," *Pew Research Center*, November 14, 2016, www .pewresearch.org/fact-tank/2016/11/14/if-the-u-s-had-100-people-charting -americans-religious-affiliations/.

[12]Jason Mandryk, *Operation World: The Definitive Prayer Guide to Every Nation*, 7th ed., (Downers Grove, IL: InterVarsity Press, 2010), 3.

[13]Daniel White Hodge, Fuller Seminary Chapel, November 1, 2017, https:// youtu.be/Rc81C86RkZc (39:15 mark).

1 STRUGGLING WITH EVANGELICALISM

[1]Jim Wallis, interview on *The Daily Show with Jon Stewart*, January 18, 2005, www.cc.com/video/gh3ctx/the-daily-show-with-jon-stewart -jim-wallis.

[2]To find out what the remaining posts were about, visit http://the commonloon.blogspot.com/2008/.

[3]*Fuller* magazine, Issue 2, Winter 2015, https://fullerstudio.fuller.edu /issue/issue-two/.

[4]Erin Dufault-Hunter, "Confessions of a Reluctant Evangelical," *Fuller*, Issue 2, Winter 2015, https://fullerstudio.fuller.edu/confessions -reluctant-evangelical/.

[5]Missio Alliance, "Distinguishing Features," www.missioalliance.org /distinguishing-features/, accessed April 15, 2021.

[6]Lots of vocab here: "New Calvinism" is the movement within conservative evangelicalism influenced by John Piper, Al Mohler, and Matt Chandler among others known for popularizing key points of Calvinist theology while insisting on complementarianism: the view that men, not women, are tasked by God with overarching leadership roles in the church and home. For a helpful reflection on the differences between New Calvinism and the Dutch neo-Calvinist tradition (also called Kuyperianism in reference to Abraham Kuyper) espoused by Richard Mouw

and James K. A. Smith, see Richard Mouw, *All That God Cares About: Common Grace and Divine Delight* (Grand Rapids, MI: Brazos Press, 2020), 136-41.

2 DEFINING EVANGELICALISM: UNDERSTANDING OUR HISTORY

[1]Jonathan Merritt, "Defining 'Evangelical,'" *The Atlantic*, December 7, 2015, www.theatlantic.com/politics/archive/2015/12/evangelical -christian/418236/.

[2]Michael Gryboski, "How Best to Define Evangelical? There Are 'Many Evangelicalisms,' Historian Says," *Christian Post*, January 8, 2019, www .christianpost.com/news/how-best-to-define-evangelical-there-are -many-evangelicalisms-historian-says.html.

[3]David W. Bebbington, *Evangelicalism in Modern Britain: A History from the 1730s to the 1980s* (London: Unwin Hyman, 1989), 2-3.

[4]Thomas S. Kidd, *Who Is an Evangelical?: The History of a Movement in Crisis* (New Haven, CT: Yale University Press, 2019), 4.

[5]Jessica Martínez and Gregory A. Smith, "How the Faithful Voted: A Preliminary 2016 Analysis," *Pew Research Center*, November 9, 2016, www.pewresearch.org/fact-tank/2016/11/09/how-the-faithful -voted-a-preliminary-2016-analysis/.

[6]Frank Newport, "Religious Group Voting and the 2020 Election," *Gallup*, November 13, 2020, https://news.gallup.com/opinion/polling-matters /324410/religious-group-voting-2020-election.aspx.

[7]Samuel Smith, "Less Than Half of US Evangelicals 'Strongly Agree' with Core Evangelical Beliefs: LifeWay," *Christian Post*, December 8, 2017, www .christianpost.com/news/less-than-half-us-evangelicals-strongly-agree -core-evangelical-beliefs-lifeway-209429/.

[8]Joseph Liu, "How the Faithful Voted: 2012 Preliminary Analysis," *Pew Research Center*, November 7, 2012, www.pewforum.org/2012/11/07 /how-the-faithful-voted-2012-preliminary-exit-poll-analysis/.

[9]*New York Times/CBS News Poll*, "How Different Groups Voted for President," *New York Times*, November 9, 1980, https://timesmachine.nytimes .com/timesmachine/1980/11/09/issue.html.

[10]Kenneth L. Woodward, "Born Again! The Year of the Evangelicals," *Newsweek*, October 25, 1976.

[11]Larry Eskridge, "Defining Evangelicalism," *Wheaton College Institute for the Study of American Evangelicals*, 2012. https://web.archive.org/web

/20160614171830/http://www.wheaton.edu/ISAE/Defining-Evangelicalism
/Defining-the-Term.

[12]T. M. Luhrmann, *When God Talks Back: Understanding the American Evangelical Relationship with God* (New York: Vintage Books, 2012), xv.

[13]Jemar Tisby, Twitter thread, June 16, 2020, https://twitter.com/JemarTisby
/status/1273015403418202112.

[14]Sarah Eekhoff Zylstra, "1 in 3 American Evangelicals Is a Person of Color," *Christianity Today*, September 6, 2017, www.christianitytoday.com/news
/2017/september/1-in-3-american-evangelicals-person-of-color-prri-atlas
.html.

[15]Daniel Cox and Robert P. Jones, "America's Changing Religious Identity," *Public Religion Research Institute*, September 6, 2017, www.prri.org
/research/american-religious-landscape-christian-religiously-unaffiliated/.

[16]Brian C. Stiller et al., *Evangelicals Around the World: A Global Handbook for the 21st Century* (Nashville: Thomas Nelson, 2015), 302.

[17]Stiller et al., *Evangelicals Around the World*, 40.

[18]"Religious Composition by Country, 2010 to 2050," *Pew Research Center*, April 2, 2015, www.pewforum.org/2015/04/02/religious-projection-table
/2020/number/all/.

[19]"Religious Composition by Country"; Stiller et al., *Evangelicals Around the World*, 40.

[20]Melani McAlister, *The Kingdom of God Has No Borders: A Global History of American Evangelicals* (New York: Oxford University Press, 2018), 207.

[21]McAlister, *The Kingdom of God Has No Borders*, 208.

[22]Jim Wallis, interview with Krista Tippett, *On Being*, November 29, 2007, https://onbeing.org/programs/jim-wallis-the-new-evangelical
-leaders-part-i/.

[23]George M. Marsden, *Reforming Fundamentalism: Fuller Seminary and the New Evangelicalism* (Grand Rapids, MI: Eerdmans, 1995), 287.

[24]Donald A. McGavran, *Understanding Church Growth* (Grand Rapids, MI: Eerdmans, 1980), 223.

[25]Brian L. Wilcox et al., "Report of the APA Task Force on Advertising and Children," *American Psychological Association*, February 20, 2004, www
.apa.org/pubs/info/reports/advertising-children.

3 FAITH STREAM AWARENESS:
KNOWING YOUR LOCATION

[1]Kate Shellnut, "A Tale of Two Calvary Chapels: Behind the Movement's Split," *Christianity Today*, February 17, 2017, www.christianitytoday.com/ct/2017/march/tale-of-two-calvary-chapel-movement-split-chuck-smith.html.

[2]Lauren Grubaugh, Twitter thread, May 7, 2018, https://twitter.com/laurengrubaugh/status/993689303887867911.

[3]Lesslie Newbigin, *Foolishness to the Greeks: The Gospel and Western Culture* (Grand Rapids, MI: Eerdmans, 1986), 4.

[4]Portions of this chapter are adapted from a seminary paper I wrote in 2015, "Individualism in American Evangelical Ecclesiology: Greatest Strength or Achilles Heel?"

[5]Tish Harrison Warren, "Why Evangelicals Should Care More About Ecclesiology," Mere Orthodoxy, August 29, 2018, https://mereorthodoxy.com/evangelical-ecclesiology-indifference/.

[6]George Hunsberger, "Evangelical Conversion Toward a Missional Ecclesiology," in *Evangelical Ecclesiology*, ed. John G. Stackhouse Jr (Grand Rapids, MI: Baker Academic, 2003), 118.

[7]For a robust list of idolatries and injustices based on misconceptions about America's identity, see Jonathan P. Walton, *Twelve Lies That Hold America Captive: And the Truth That Sets Us Free* (Downers Grove, IL: InterVarsity Press, 2019).

[8]Dan Stringer, "7 Churches in 9 Days," *Dan Stringer* (blog), August 22, 2012, www.danstringer.net/2012/08/22/7-churches-in-9-days/.

[9]Dan Stringer, "Evangelicals in Hawaii: How Are We Different?" *The Common Loon* (blog), October 8, 2009, http://thecommonloon.blogspot.com/2009/10/evangelicals-in-hawaii-how-are-we.html.

4 WHY APPRECIATION MATTERS

[1]"Global Christianity," Pew Research Center, December 1, 2014, www.pewforum.org/interactives/global-christianity/.

[2]Evangelical Covenant Church Affirmations, https://covchurch.org/who-we-are/beliefs/affirmations/.

[3]See Dennis Saleebey, *The Strengths Perspective in Social Work Practice* (Boston: Pearson, 2012). Also https://today.ku.edu/2020/03/30/new-book-celebrates-strength-perspectives-pervasive-influence-social-work-freely.

5 STRENGTHENING OUR STRENGTHS

[1]Personal communication.

[2]Emily McFarlan Miller, Alejandra Molina, and Roxanne Stone, "At Nationwide Rallies, Christians Stand Up for Asian Americans," *Religion News Service*, March 29, 2021, https://religionnews.com/2021/03/29/christian-led-rallies-across-the-country-take-a-stand-for-asian-american-lives-amid-rising-racism/.

[3]Asian American Christian Collaborative press release, March 24, 2021, https://static1.squarespace.com/static/5e9e74aea07dbc6724a2189e/t/605e0f380c88c64bbb3b1b36/1616777016285/AACC%2BStand%2Bfor%2BAAPI%2BLives%2BRally%2B-%2BPress%2BRelease.pdf.

[4]SueJeanne Koh, "Asian American Christian Theology: Topographies, Trajectories, and Possibilities," *Religion Compass*, July 2020, https://doi.org/10.1111/rec3.12373.

[5]Tim Tseng, "A Church for Us," *Inheritance*, July 19, 2019, www.inheritancemag.com/stories/a-church-for-us.

[6]Robert Chao Romero, *Conversing* podcast by Fuller Studio, episode 79, August 25, 2020, 9:25 mark, https://fullerstudio.fuller.edu/podcast/robert-chao-romero-on-the-brown-church/.

[7]Kelefa Sanneh, "The Hell-Raiser: A Megachurch Pastor's Search for a More Forgiving Faith," *The New Yorker*, November 26, 2012.

6 EVIL CLOAKED IN SPIRITUAL LANGUAGE

[1]"A Litany," Urbana 18 (video), https://urbana.org/message/litany.

[2]Mark Charles and Soong-Chan Rah, *Unsettling Truths: The Ongoing, Dehumanizing Legacy of the Doctrine of Discovery* (Downers Grove, IL: InterVarsity Press, 2019), 194.

[3]Rich Villodas, Twitter, July 17, 2020, https://twitter.com/richvillodas/status/1284227053697617920.

[4]Mark Noll, "The Rise of the Evangelicals," *Christianity Today*, August 8, 2008, www.christianitytoday.com/history/2008/august/rise-of-evangelicals.html.

[5]Dan Snow, "DR Congo: Cursed by Its Natural Wealth," *BBC News Magazine*, October 9, 2013, www.bbc.com/news/magazine-24396390.

[6]Iolani Palace visitor website, www.iolanipalace.org/.

[7]David W. Forbes (ed.), *The Diaries of Queen Liliuokalani of Hawaii* (Honolulu: Hui Hānai, 2019), 433-51.

[8]Forbes, *The Diaries of Queen Lilinuokalani*, 458-507.

[9]Moanikeʻala Nanod-Sitch, personal communication with author, April 12, 2021.

7 LEARNING TO REPENT COMMUNALLY

[1]Portions of this section were adapted from Dan Stringer, "Pulling Teeth," in *Father Factor: American Christian Men on Fatherhood and Faith*, ed. R. Anderson Campbell (Ashland, OR: White Cloud Press, 2014), 6-12.

[2]Michael O. Emerson and Christian Smith, *Divided by Faith: Evangelical Religion and the Problem of Race in America* (New York: Oxford University Press, 2000), 75-76.

[3]Jemar Tisby, *The Color of Compromise: The Truth About the American Church's Complicity in Racism* (Grand Rapids, MI: Zondervan, 2019), 176.

[4]Emerson and Smith, *Divided by Faith*, 76-77.

[5]Emerson and Smith, *Divided by Faith*, 79.

[6]Tisby, *The Color of Compromise*, 175.

[7]Mae Elise Cannon, Lisa Sharon Harper, Troy Jackson, and Soong-Chan Rah, *Forgive Us: Confessions of a Compromised Faith* (Grand Rapids, MI: Zondervan, 2014), 30.

[8]Tommy Givens, New Testament course notes, Fuller Seminary, Winter 2015.

[9]Sandra Maria Van Opstal, "Remaining to Reform" in *Still Evangelical? Insiders Consider Political, Social, and Theological Meaning*, edited by Mark Labberton (Downers Grove, IL: InterVarsity Press, 2018), 130.

[10]Van Opstal, "Remaining to Reform," 132.

[11]Mark Charles and Soong-Chan Rah, *Unsettling Truths: The Ongoing, Dehumanizing Legacy of the Doctrine of Discovery* (Downers Grove, IL: InterVarsity Press, 2019), 186.

[12]Hill's reflections on this episode appear in Daniel Hill, *White Awake* (Downers Grove, IL: InterVarsity Press, 2017), chapter 8. See also https://covenantcompanion.com/2015/12/09/covenant-pastor-receives-threatening-email-following-prayer/.

8 IS EVANGELICALISM WORTH RENEWING?

[1]Lance is a composite character of real people but with details changed.

[2]For a helpful summary of purity culture, see Rachel Joy Welcher, *Talking Back to Purity Culture* (Downers Grove, IL: InterVarsity Press, 2020), 16.

[3]Using Matthew 5:22 as an example, the NRSV, CEB, and NIV (since 2011) accurately translate the Greek word *adelphos* as *brother* or *sister* in this context, whereas translations like the ESV, NKJV, and NASB translate it as *brother*. The NLT and CEV broaden it to say *someone*. My practice is to avoid the ESV, NKJV, and NASB when leading Bible study groups or when selecting Scriptures to be read aloud. For more on why this matters, see

Gail Wallace, "4 Reasons to Use a Gender Accurate Translation," *Christians for Biblical Equality*, December 4, 2017, www.cbeinternational.org /resource/article/mutuality-blog-magazine/4-reasons-use-gender -accurate-bible-translation.

[4]Jemar Tisby, *The Color of Compromise: The Truth About the American Church's Complicity in Racism* (Grand Rapids, MI: Zondervan, 2019), 39.

[5]Michelle A. Clifton-Soderstrom, Paul H. DeNeui, and Soong-Chan Rah, "A Commitment to the Whole Mission of the Church" in *Living Faith: Reflections on Covenant Affirmations*, edited by James K. Bruckner et al. (Chicago: Covenant Publications, 2010), 83.

[6]Tisby, *Color of Compromise*, 204-5.

[7]Tisby, *Color of Compromise*, 214.

[8]Chrissy Stroop and Lauren O'Neal (eds.), *Empty the Pews: Stories of Leaving the Church* (Indianapolis: Epiphany Publishing, 2019).

9 BETTER THAN WE FOUND IT

[1]Jemar Tisby, *The Color of Compromise: The Truth About the American Church's Complicity in Racism* (Grand Rapids, MI: Zondervan, 2019), 20.

[2]Tisby, *Color of Compromise*, 66.

[3]Rebecca Solnit, *Hope in the Dark: Untold Histories, Wild Possibilities* (Edinburgh: Canongate Books, 2016), xiv.

[4]Mae Elise Cannon, Lisa Sharon Harper, Troy Jackson, and Soong-Chan Rah, *Forgive Us: Confessions of a Compromised Faith* (Grand Rapids, MI: Zondervan, 2014), 206.

[5]Makoto Fujimura, *Culture Care: Reconnecting with Beauty for our Common Life* (Downers Grove, IL: InterVarsity Press, 2017), 24.

[6]Fujimura, *Culture Care*, 40.

[7]Philip B. Payne, *Man and Woman, One in Christ: An Exegetical and Theological Study of Paul's Letters* (Grand Rapids, MI: Zondervan, 2009).

[8]www.churchclarity.org

[9]For more on the Side A versus Side B framework and how it came about, see Justin Lee, *Torn: Rescuing the Gospel from the Gays-vs.-Christians Debate* (New York: Jericho Books, 2012), 221-24.

[10]David Neff, "Together in the Jesus Story," *Christianity Today*, September 1, 2006, www.christianitytoday.com/ct/2006/september/10.54.html.

EPILOGUE: HOPE FOR YOUR STRUGGLE

[1]Erin Dufault-Hunter, "Confessions of a Reluctant Evangelical," *Fuller*, Issue 2, Winter 2015, https://fullerstudio.fuller.edu/confessions-reluctant -evangelical/.

ABOUT THE AUTHOR

DAN STRINGER GREW UP as a third culture kid in five countries on three continents. He is a graduate of Wheaton College and Fuller Theological Seminary, ordained in the Evangelical Covenant Church, and serves as team leader for InterVarsity's Graduate and Faculty Ministries in Hawai'i.

Dan is pastor of theological formation at Wellspring Covenant Church in Hālawa, Hawai'i. He previously was a social worker helping people obtain housing and employment. He has written for Missio Alliance, Inheritance, and Level Ground, and is a contributor to Father Factor.

Connect with Dan:

Twitter: @revdanstringer

Facebook: @revdanstringer

Instagram: @revdanstringer

www.danstringer.net